WITHDRAWN
UTSA LIBRARIES

MARTIN ZAUSNER is Executive Vice President of Arthur Schmidt & Associates, Inc., a financial relations consulting firm. He received his M.S. from Columbia University and M.B.A. from New York University. Mr. Zausner has an extensive background in financial relations and, earlier, as an investment advisor.

CORPORATE POLICY

AND THE

INVESTMENT COMMUNITY

MARTIN ZAUSNER

ARTHUR SCHMIDT & ASSOCIATES, INC.

THE RONALD PRESS COMPANY · NEW YORK

Copyright © 1968 by
THE RONALD PRESS COMPANY

———————

All Rights Reserved

No part of this book may be reproduced
in any form without permission in writing
from the publisher.

Library of Congress Catalog Card Number: 68–13476

PRINTED IN THE UNITED STATES OF AMERICA

Preface

The company that takes the initiative to elicit Wall Street's understanding can command a good share of its attention. However, because so few publicly owned companies conduct a well-conceived and properly executed investor relations program, a great many fail to get the attention they deserve from the investment community. This is not surprising if one considers the many thousands of companies competing for Wall Street recognition. It is impossible for the relatively few security analysts in the country—many of whom duplicate each other's work—to ferret out each of the 25,000 publicly owned companies for critical review on a continuing basis.

In the author's experience, most company presidents, although usually reticent about discussing the price of their company's stock, will eventually confide that the price should be a little higher than its then current level. Surprisingly enough, that attitude generally holds true whether the stock is selling at ten, twenty, or thirty times its per-share earnings.

What each of these executives is really saying is that the investment community is undervaluing his company, that if Wall Street understood the situation as well as it should, the stock would sell at a higher price.

If the investment community does not understand a company, it is probably more the fault of that company than of anyone else. The responsibility for properly informing investors and their advisors about a company lies with the company itself. The task is a major and highly technical one, a substantial part

of which involves working with security analysts on a professional level. The difficulties of this undertaking are apparent
when one examines the work load of the typical security analyst. Although he normally specializes in two or three industries,
even in the instance where he is responsible for only one industry it is usually beyond his capacity to stay sufficiently informed
to make valid investment decisions about all companies within
his sphere of responsibility. Certainly he will try to keep abreast
of developments in the largest companies; but smaller ones,
and this can mean companies with sales well over $100 million,
must initiate the effort to keep him regularly informed about
the company's plans, programs, and progress.

The purpose of this book is to explain what management
must do, on a continuing basis, to develop and implement a
well-rounded investor-relations program that takes into consideration the company's internal actions and its dialogues with
the professional investment community, its stockholders, and
the financial press. At stake in the conduct of such a program
is recognition from the investment community that accurately
reflects a company's present status and future prospects.

There are many who contributed their time, advice, and
criticism to this book. I am especially grateful to my wife,
Adrienne B. Zausner, a member of the investment banking firm
of Dominick & Dominick, Inc., who gave me many valuable
comments and suggestions and also served as grammarian and
proofreader. The debt I owe to Robert B. Menschel, a partner
of Goldman, Sachs & Co., is immeasurable. Many of the ideas
expressed in this book are an outgrowth of our discussions—
begun when we were in college together and still continuing—
concerning the developing role of the corporation in relation
to the investment community.

My thanks and appreciation go to my associates, Arthur A.
Schmidt and Robert B. Mackall, who encouraged me to write
this book and to my colleagues, Michael Osheowitz and Alan S
Weinstein for their critical and professional evaluation of the
manuscript as it went through its various drafts. My thanks

also to John Kirk for his editorial assistance and to my secretary, Rochelle P. Kenny, for the hours she spent taking dictation and typing the many revisions.

MARTIN ZAUSNER

New York, New York
   January, 1968

Contents

CONTENTS

CORPORATE POLICY

AND THE

INVESTMENT COMMUNITY

1

Scope of Investment
Community Relations

Among the more important objectives of a financial relations program are:

1. Increasing the number and geographic spread of stockholders
2. Increasing the trading activity of the stock
3. Strengthening stockholder loyalty to the company, its products, and its long-term goals
4. Obtaining sponsorship from leading brokerage firms and banks
5. Developing institutional investor interest
6. Creating a favorable climate for the acquisition of other companies
7. Making the company more attractive to present and potential key management personnel

One objective that a financial relations program should *not* have is to increase the price of a company's stock. In a well-conducted program, where the proper information is given out in the right manner, at the right time, to the right people, the price will reflect its own fair market level.

The study of a company's financial relations activities may be divided into four specific areas: the company's internal policies,

3

the professional investment community, stockholders, and the
financial press. Policies and procedures must be developed
for each of these areas. Once this has been done, routine questions—such as whether the company should increase its regular
dividend rather than pay a year-end extra, or how much
information ought to be disclosed to a security analyst, or how
to handle an annual meeting, or what to announce to the financial press—will be easily answered.

Each of these four segments is important, but a company's
internal financial actions, or lack of them, speak louder than
its considered financial communications. Next in order of
importance is the relationship with the professional investment
community, primarily the security analysts. It is the analysts
who receive and interpret corporate financial information. It
is their opinion that is acted upon, whether by the institutional
or the individual investor.

FORMULATION OF INTERNAL POLICY

The most important factors in a company's relationship with
the investment community grow out of policies and practices
that often are not considered to have a bearing on its investor
relations program. Relatively few executives are aware of what
the effect will be on the investment community when their
company raises capital, utilizes its surplus cash, determines
when to split its shares, or sets its general dividend policy.

Many companies narrowly define their stockholder and
financial relations program as one of communications with
stockholders, security analysts, and the financial press. Yet,
before the first report is sent to a stockholder, the first talk
held with a security analyst, or the first news announcement
issued to the press, the financial stature of the company may
already have been determined.

To some extent, a company's internal actions will determine
the type of investor who becomes a stockholder. Such factors
as the price at which a stock sells, where it is listed, and how
many institutions own it all work to channel individual investors towards one company and away from another. Even

a company's name can be an influential factor in attracting or discouraging stockholders.

The way management handles internal affairs can determine its vulnerability in a proxy contest. Some companies permit themselves to become susceptible to raiders while others develop barriers to make any take-over difficult.

Internal auditing and reporting practices can influence the investment community's attitude. Companies that have developed procedures for assessing and reporting results soon after the close of a period are apt to make a more favorable impression on and receive more attention from security analysts, stockholders, and the press than those who take long to collect and issue financial data.

Place of Financial Relations in Corporate Planning. Despite the critical need for consideration of the impact of internal policy on the investing public, many companies limit the duties of their investor relations staff or outside financial relations counseling firm to little more than reporting and interpreting the company's activities. Seldom does their responsibility include the more fundamental function of participating in the formulation of internal policies that affect the investment community.

The impact of internal corporate decisions on financial relations must always be taken into account, but this does not mean that it must be the determining factor. The weight that it is given must be in proportion to all other corporate objectives. Unpopular decisions, such as a financing that may temporarily reduce earnings, may sometimes have to be made. A company that has developed an effective investor relations program and has always considered the investment community when formulating internal policies should be able to count on the community's support when such a decision is necessary.

THE PROFESSIONAL INVESTMENT COMMUNITY

Security analysts probably play the most important role in determining which stocks are purchased by individuals and institutions. The relatively small group of individuals—probably not many more than 10,000—engaged in security analysis has become almost the dominant segment of the investment community. Once neglected, its authority has expanded at an astonishing pace in the last two decades. Any company concerned about relations with the investing public must pay careful attention to its relations with those professionally active in finance—particularly the security analysts.

Competition for Analysts' Attention. Thousands and thousands of companies, listed and unlisted, vie for the attention of the investment community. Although efforts have been made by research staffs to divide these companies into industry segments so that they are easier to follow, the number of companies involved is enough to overwhelm any security research department.

Many security analysts are expected to be familiar with and report on more than 100 companies in their fields of specialization. This is an almost impossible task. The amount of time and attention that an analyst can devote to companies other than the most important leaders in an industry is necessarily limited. Even companies with sales of half a billion dollars or more are sometimes neglected.

The smaller the company, the more effort it must make to attract the attention of the financial community. This does not mean that it should be over-aggressive in the conduct of its financial relations program. On the contrary, to be effective a financial relations program must be soundly and conservatively conceived and executed.

Strategy. Although the investment field is relatively concentrated, it is still too large and unwieldy for companies to reach every area. Companies must single out the specific individuals, firms, and institutions that will be most influential in the development of the financial community's attitudes towards the company.

To execute such a program properly requires a full-time effort on a continual basis. Company executives must take the initiative in contacts with members of the financial community. They must see that there is proper flow of financial information and make certain that analysts' requests for information are promptly and adequately filled.

Analysts pride themselves on being objective. Many claim that they judge a company's worth and its management's abilities solely by statistics. This is rarely true. Analysts are impressed by a well-presented and well-written document, an enthusiastic executive, or a dynamic speech and tend to downgrade a company that does not present itself in an appealing manner. The *manner* in which a presentation is made is an important factor, as well as the content.

STOCKHOLDERS

The rapid growth in the number of stockholders has brought many benefits to corporations. However, as the stockholder ranks have swelled, the percentage of stockholders with little investment knowledge has increased rapidly. Almost half of all the more than 20 million stockholders in America have had no college education, and a substantial portion of the remainder have never had a finance or economics course.

No matter how effective a communications job a company does, a large proportion of its stockholders will not fully comprehend the company's financial affairs. This places a difficult burden on the company. In effect, the company is forced to communicate with stockholders in a manner enabling as large a percentage as possible to understand what the company is trying to tell them. In addition, the company must help further their financial education.

Financial Terminology. One of the problems in communicating with stockholders is that financial terminology is like a foreign language to many people. Words that most executives assume are part of everyone's vocabulary are incomprehensible to many stockholders. For example, surveys have shown that more than half of all stockholders cannot define inflation any better than "rising prices" and are thoroughly in the dark with such technical phrases as depletion allowances and operating revenues.

The answer is *not* to resort to reducing financial reports to a level appropriate for an eighth-grader. This will only antagonize the professionals who are also vitally interested in stockholder communications. There is no ideal solution, and admittedly the line that a company must walk in communicating with its stockholders is a fine one. A presentation that is either too technical or too simple will send readers scurrying off.

Stockholder Dependence on Investment Counsel. Their basic lack of financial knowledge accounts for stockholders' great reliance on others for investment counsel. Typically, a stock purchase can be traced to professional advice. This does not mean that there are no other influences. Certainly, many stockholders purchase stocks merely because they "like a company." This is often the case with companies that have heavily advertised consumer products.

Stockholder Loyalty. Once a stockholder purchases stock in a particular company, he can become tenacious about his investment and extremely loyal to the company. Although his decision to purchase a stock may have originated with a stock market professional, he will not necessarily sell merely because the same individual tells him to. Owning American Telephone and Telegraph Company shares, for example, is almost a religion to many stockholders, not an investment. If every A.T.&T. stockholder were to receive a sell recommendation from his broker on a given day, chances are that the number that would heed such advice would be small indeed.

An important goal of an investor relations program is to build loyalties of this kind. When a stockholder has confidence in a company he tends to be a missionary for it. He prefers to buy that company's products and will often tell his friends to do so. He will also recommend the stock to them as an investment.

The main investment objective of almost all stockholders is

price appreciation. Certainly stockholders like to receive dividends; but, more important, they want profits. This means that it is nearly impossible for all of a company's stockholders to be completely satisfied at all times. Whenever a stock is selling below its high, there must be some stockholders who have a loss on their purchase. A company must develop a relationship with its stockholders that will keep their loyalty through adverse times as well as during normal business periods.

THE FINANCIAL PRESS

The financial press is important as part of an overall investor relations program. As an isolated segment, its influence on determining stock selection has been greatly exaggerated.

Rarely does an investor make a decision to buy a stock on the basis of a story or article he has read about a company. A news story—or the cumulative effect of many stories—may lead a potential investor to make inquiries of his stockbroker as to the investment merits of a company. Generally, however, financial stories tend to play an influential role in subtler ways. As a factor in stock selection, they can:

1. Acquaint a potential investor with a company so that he is favorably pre-conditioned to follow his broker's advice to invest in that company
2. Stimulate action on the part of an investor who was already considering an investment in that company
3. Reinforce, to a current stockholder, the soundness of his investment
4. Influence a current stockholder, who was considering the sale of his shares, to reappraise the situation

The amount of space devoted to business and financial stories has been keeping pace with the growth of public participation in the stock market. In addition to the growing circulation of financial and investment publications—such as the *Wall Street Journal, Barrons,* and *Forbes*—newspapers and general magazines have been increasing their coverage of the business field.

To take advantage of the increased interest in business and financial news, a company must round out its investor relations program by developing policies and procedures relating to the financial press that fit into the framework of the other elements of its investment community relations program.

I

INTERNAL CORPORATE POLICY

2

Dividend Policy

There is probably no specific action that a company can take that affects its stockholders more directly and more immediately than a dividend declaration—whether it be of cash or stock. A company's dividend policy plays a major role in establishing its character in the minds of the investment community. The impact of dividend policy usually is felt in two major areas: the type of investors attracted as stockholders and the price action of the company's stock.

Whatever dividend policy a company finally adopts, the policy, and the reasons behind it, should be carefully explained to stockholders. Companies that follow this practice almost always obtain stockholder support and approval for their dividend actions.

CASH DIVIDENDS

It is not the purpose of this Chapter to discuss how large or how small the cash dividend of a company should be. The company's earnings growth, current cash situation, cash flow, and future cash requirements and the nature of its business are the primary determinants of the size of its dividend. However, after these factors are taken into consideration, a great deal of flexibility is still possible in setting and executing dividend policy.

Dividend Consistency. Dividend consistency is important to all stockholders, and especially to those who have purchased the stock primarily because of the strength of its dividends—and the implication that such dividends will be maintained. Many of these stockholders need dividends as part of their income, and a company must recognize its responsibility to such investors. Further, the reputation in the financial community of a company that cuts dividends suffers drastically.

A company should, therefore, set its dividend rate so that it can be reasonably certain of being able to maintain payments at that level. The amount of dividend payments should be based on earnings expectations over future years, not merely the current year. The level should be set so that the payments can be maintained despite typical earning fluctuations. However, there is a point where a company may become too conservative. A rate that is set ridiculously low just to insure the ability to maintain it reflects neither good management nor sound dividend practice.

Most companies determine their dividends by the percentage of earnings they would like to pay out. Whether this is 30 per cent or 70 per cent of earnings, it should be used as a fairly stable general guide and not as something that must be adjusted on a year-to-year basis. The average percentage payout over several years should be given more weight than the payment ratio in any one year.

Dividend Continuity. A key factor that a company should consider in its dividend policy is the continuity record of its dividend payments. Stockholders look unfavorably on companies with dividend-payment records that show occasional payment omissions and tend to suspect the present dividend rate of any company whose history of dividend payouts has been erratic. In the main, stockholders—especially those who are income oriented—like to invest in companies with a long history of consecutive years of dividend payments.

While there may be times when a company will have to consider omitting payment of dividends because of deficits and poor cash position, such drastic action should be avoided whenever possible. A deficit is not always sufficient reason to omit a dividend payment. If the company's outlook is not desperate in terms of future earnings expectations, or there is no dire need to conserve its cash, dividends may still be appropriate during temporary periods of loss operations.

As a last resort, a token dividend paid during the course of the year can prove important to a company in later years. Such a token dividend may enable the company to report— some years later—that it has paid annual dividends *without interruption* for, say, two decades.

Of course, a company should not pay cash dividends if this might jeopardize its stockholders' investment. Obviously, all factors must be weighed in deciding whether or not to eliminate dividend payments for an entire year.

Size of Dividends. In most instances, the determining factor in setting the percentage of corporate earnings that will be paid out in dividends is the company's near-term capital requirements. However—and quite paradoxically—companies that frequently have to raise substantial sums of capital, such as utilities, have found great success using a *high* dividend payout rather than a low one. A high payout attracts a large and faithful group of stockholders who are anxious to participate in rights offerings when additional capital is needed.

Frequency of Dividends. Whenever possible, dividends should be declared regularly—preferably on a quarterly basis. One reason is that many stockholders rely on dividends for current expenses and need the money at frequent intervals. The benefits a company receives from paying dividends will be lessened by semi-annual or annual payments.

A few companies have found that monthly dividends are welcomed by their stockholders. The experience of these companies is that the relatively small additional expense of monthly payments is justified in terms of their stockholders' satisfaction and loyalty.

Extra Dividends.   Investors place less value on extra dividends than they do on regular dividends. They do not usually consider the extras to be a permanent part of the company's dividend, and yields are often calculated on the basis of the regular dividend only. On the other hand, if a customary extra dividend is reduced or eliminated without a corresponding change in the regular dividend rate, the reaction can be as adverse as if the reduction were made in a regular dividend payment. Therefore, for companies with fairly steady income, there is little justification for paying extra dividends rather than raising the regular dividend rate.

Increasing the Dividend.   If stockholders like to receive dividends, they like to receive dividend *increases* even more. Many companies try to increase their dividend payments each year. Such consistency inspires investor confidence in future growth and is rewarded by a high appraisal placed on the value of a company's stock. Typical of the companies that have records of consistent dividend increases are: Addressograph-Multigraph Corporation, Beech-Nut Life Savers, Inc., Eastman Kodak Company, Florida Power & Light Company, General Telephone & Electronics Corporation, International Business Machines Corporation, Plough, Inc., Texas Utilities Company, Upjohn Company, Virginia Electric & Power Company, and Warner-Lambert Pharmaceutical Company.

Dividend Timing.   Many companies unwittingly forego the opportunity to establish a prestige-building dividend record of year-after-year increases because of *incorrectly timed* increases.

A company that increases its dividend with the first payment of the year must do so every year to maintain a continuous record of annual increased dividends. However, a company that increases its dividend in any period other than the first need increase its dividend only every *second* year to show a record of annual dividend increases. This occurs because the full effect of the increase is not present until the following year—the first complete year to which it applies. This difference can result in one company having a superior dividend record and another company only an average one, even though both increased their dividend rate by the same amount and as frequently.

As an example, consider a company that is going to raise its quarterly dividend from 20 cents to 30 cents per share. Instead of raising the quarterly dividend in the year's first quarter, the company sets the increase for the third quarter of the year. The result is two years of increased dividends. In the preceding complete year the total annual dividend was 80 cents (20 cents in each quarter). In the first year in which the increase is introduced, the total annual dividend will be $1.00 (20 cents in each of the first two quarters, and 30 cents in each of the last two). For the year following the introduction of the increase —the first year in which the increase applies to all four quarters—the total annual dividend will be $1.20 (30 cents in each quarter).

The table in Fig. 2–1 illustrates how a pattern of annual increases can be established through introduction of a quarterly increase in the third quarter of every other year. It also shows the irregular effect of introducing the same increases in the first quarter.

| | | Total Annual Dividend When Increase Occurs as of: | |
Year	Quarterly Dividend Rate	Third Quarter	First Quarter
1st	20¢	.80	.80
2nd	Increased to 30¢	1.00	1.20
3rd	30¢	1.20	1.20
4th	Increased to 40¢	1.40	1.60
5th	40¢	1.60	1.60
6th	Increased to 50¢	1.80	2.00
7th	50¢	2.00	2.00
8th	Increased to 60¢	2.20	2.40
9th	60¢	2.40	2.40

Fig. 2–1. Pattern of Annual Dividend Increases

Cutting a Dividend.   Reducing a dividend is one of the most unpleasant tasks a board of directors has to perform. As a result, it is often done with too much timidity, which aggravates rather than helps a difficult situation.

If a dividend must be cut, the situation should be faced immediately and realistically. To delay the decision to pare a dividend helps neither the company nor its stockholders. Even before the dividend cut is announced, the stock will probably have dropped substantially because the investment community will more than likely be aware of the conditions that make the cut necessary.

The total amount of the cut should be determined and made all at one time. It is much better to have one substantial dividend cut—and get the bad news out of the way—than to reduce the dividend in several agonizing stages.

On the other hand, as stated earlier, if a declining profit situation seems reasonably certain to be a temporary one, a company with a sound balance sheet should not panic and cut the dividend merely because it is not covered by current earnings for a short period.

Dividend Restrictions. Corporate borrowing usually brings with it certain restrictions on dividends. This is particularly true when borrowing from institutional lenders which may impose severer terms on the company than those incurred through a public debt issue. Occasionally, such restrictions can dictate the company's normal dividend policy.

Directors should feel reasonably certain that the company will be able to meet the minimum requirements demanded by the lenders and at the same time maintain its dividend. If it cannot, they should re-examine the need for this money and weigh the return the company will be able to make on it against the long-range effect that decreased or discontinued dividends will have on its stockholder relations and financial record.

STOCK DIVIDENDS

It is the rare company that will benefit from paying a stock dividend. This belief is in conflict with the popular opinion that stock dividends are beneficial.

Management, for example, usually believes that it is capitalizing earnings and creating good stockholder relations when it issues a stock dividend. In fact, management may be reducing the market value of the stock and at the same time upsetting stockholder relations.

Stockholders often believe that they are getting free shares of stock and that the market value of their original shares will automatically and quickly return to its pre-dividend level. In fact, the stockholder gets little more than a psychological lift and a few more pieces of paper which do not increase the value of his holdings in the company.

Yet, stock dividends have been on the increase since the 1920 Supreme Court decision that ruled that such dividends were not taxable as income. More than 10 times the number of corporations that issued stock dividends in 1944 (13) did so a few years ago.

Definition. The New York Stock Exchange classifies as stock dividends any distribution of shares amounting to 24 per cent or less of the shares then outstanding. Anything larger is termed a stock split. Similarly, the American Institute of Certified Public Accountants considers the dividing line between stock dividends and stock splits to be 20 to 25 per cent of the shares outstanding. Most stock dividends are less than 10 per cent, clustering in the 3 to 5 per cent area—the range that is chiefly under discussion here.

Fallacies Concerning Stock Dividends. There are a number of misconceptions current as to the benefits of stock dividends:

1. *Stock dividends help a company conserve cash.* In fact, the do not, although this is the rationalization whenever a company uses a stock dividend in lieu of all or part of a cash dividend. The company could have conserved just as much cash without paying a stock dividend. In essence, the stock dividend is used as a *psychological substitute* for cash. Effective communications between the company and its shareholders can do much more than a stock dividend in making a stockholder content with a low cash disbursement.

2. *Stock dividends broaden stock ownership.* In fact, it is

nearly impossible to determine whether or not a small stock dividend does broaden the base of share ownership. If the stock dividend does increase the number of stockholders, the extent of the increase and the time it takes to make itself felt have not been discernible. Undoubtedly, a company that pays small stock dividends for many years will eventually greatly increase the number of shares in the floating supply, which will result in an increase in share ownership. But if a company really wants to broaden its stock ownership, it ought to split its stock. A stock split is a far more effective device, as is shown below (page 22).

3. *Stock dividends are a good way to give small increases in the cash dividend.* In fact, the value of the insignificant cash increase that comes from maintaining the same dividend rate when paying small stock dividends is highly questionable. It is better to increase the regular cash dividend and build a dividend record that shows frequent—even if small—increases.

4. *Stock dividends increase the stock's price.* In fact, studies have shown that permanent price gains in the company's stock came only when the stock dividend was accompanied by an increase in the cash dividend. Almost without exception, the stocks of companies that had declared stock dividends *only* sold lower in relation to the general market six months later.

The prime determinants of the market value of a stock are profits and the outlook for future profits and perhaps its cash dividend paying ability. *Stock dividends do not affect these factors.*

The *temporary* effect of stock dividends on the price action of a stock is a different situation. Rumors of a forthcoming stock dividend may increase the price of the stock, and the ultimate distribution itself may result in a quick rise in the stock's price. But such a rapid increase is short-lived.

Other Drawbacks of Stock Dividends. For Statistical Services. Some statistical services do not adjust per share figures for small stock dividends. This means that dividends and earnings per share may be reported on a basis that will give security analysts and other investors who use these services a poorer picture of the company's earnings and dividend history than is actually the case. A company with a good growth record that regularly declares stock dividends may appear to have a relatively flat earnings picture if no adjustments have been made.

For SECURITY ANALYSTS. Even if the picture reported by the statistical services is adjusted, the security analysts may have their own problems. Their files will show earnings of past quarters as they were reported. They will not be adjusted. With the number of companies that a security analyst must follow, he cannot be expected to remember every small stock dividend and may give his firm's clients an inaccurate estimate by using unadjusted figures.

For THE COMPANY. Stock dividends can be a clerical nuisance for the company, and an expensive one at that. The company must be prepared to deal with fractional shares. Cash in lieu of fractional certificates must be paid or scrip issued so that stockholders can sell it or purchase enough additional scrip to make a full share.

For COMPANY EXECUTIVES. Executives often have difficulty in readjusting earnings of their companies in their own minds for stock dividends. When discussing earnings with security analysts, they often have to refer to documents in order to be able to talk about past results or may even forget to make the adjustment.

For THE STOCKHOLDER. One of the arguments used in favor of stock dividends is that it is easy for a stockholder to sell the additional shares that he receives. Actually such a sale creates problems for the average stockholder from a tax liability viewpoint. The money obtained from selling a stock dividend and an equivalent percentage of his total holdings if no such dividend were paid is identical. However, if a stockholder were to sell off a portion of his original holdings he would use his actual cost basis to determine his capital gain. To find his capital gain on shares on which a stock dividend was paid, he must use a dilution factor carried out to several decimal points to arrive at the average cost of his shares. For example, to determine cost per share after receiving a four per cent stock dividend, the original cost must be multiplied by .961538 to obtain the new cost basis.

FOR TRUST DEPARTMENTS. Stock dividends have disadvantages for bank trust departments, investment advisors, and brokers. They cause additional bookkeeping, storage, and clerical problems involved in keeping track of such disbursements. In addition, trust officers are faced with the uncertain legal problems of how to handle stock dividends in terms of keeping them as part of the trust or distributing them to the beneficiaries.

STOCK SPLITS

The number of companies that split their stock in any one year has been consistently increasing. This has been brought about by higher stock prices resulting from rising earnings, and the pressure for broader stock ownership.

While splitting a stock holds many benefits for a company, there are factors that should be considered before splitting. What should the timing be? How can the size of the split be best determined? What side effects go along with splitting? And, when should a stock be split?

Why Companies Split Their Stock. The decision to split a stock may be made for a number of reasons. These include:

1. *To broaden ownership.* The most important reason for a company to split its stock is to broaden ownership—to get the stock into the hands of as many stockholders as possible. Caterpillar Tractor Company, as one illustration, in a ten-year period in which its stock was split three times, more than doubled the number of its shareholders of record.

2. *To widen brokerage interest.* Brokerage firms are reluctant to recommend a stock that has a small number of shares

available for purchase by the public. Many large firms refuse to publish a report about a company unless the company has a certain minimum *number* of shares in public hands.

3. *To attract institutional interest.* The more shares a company has outstanding, the less likely it is that its capitalization will prove a barrier to an institutional purchase of stock. More important, the greater the number of shares that are in public hands, the larger the institution a company can attract. Institutions always consider the number of shares outstanding before making a decision to purchase stock in a particular company.

4. *To make underwriting easier.* Lower-priced stocks are often easier to underwrite than those that sell at high levels. In some instances, an underwriter will insist that a company split its stock prior to an underwriting.

5. *To keep stock price realistic.* One obvious purpose of companies in splitting their stock is to keep the price from eventually climbing into the hundreds or thousands of dollars —far out of the grasp of most investors.

6. *To reduce public criticism.* Splitting a stock obviously reduces per share earnings and dividends. Although this does not alter total earnings and dividends, and only a financially naive person would judge a company's profitability on the size of per share amounts, splitting a stock can help to reduce public criticism. High per-share figures have been used by groups trying to influence labor, government regulatory agencies, and others concerned with a corporation's profitability as arguments claiming a company was making exorbitant profits. For example, a utility earning, say, $30 a share is far more susceptible to criticism by groups demanding rate reductions than is the same company earning $3 a share following a ten-for-one split.

Factors Affecting Timing of Split.   There are several factors that determine the proper time to split a stock. Among these are:

HIGH STOCK PRICE.   Companies that have stocks selling at $50 and over should consider themselves candidates for a stock split. Even companies whose shares sell lower—say at $30 to $50—should consider splitting their stock if a thin market exists. If a two-for-one split is impractical, a smaller split may be justified.

Some companies like to keep their stock at high levels. The stock of International Business Machines Corporation generally sells in the $300 to $500 range, and even when IBM splits its stock, the split is rarely large enough to make the price of the shares fall below this level. There is a certain prestige attached to a higher priced stock, but prestige should never outweigh the advantages of having an active and liquid market.

The ideal price at which a stock should sell is a matter of custom. In England, for example, most stocks sell in the $5 range and are split when they rise above $10. In the United States, mutual funds usually try to have their shares sell well below the $20 level—preferably somewhere near $10. However, according to the New York Stock Exchange, studies "tend to indicate that, as a general matter, the most favorable price level for listed stocks is in the range of $18 to $25." [1] This favored price range undoubtedly changes as the market goes through its various cycles, and a price of $20 to $30 a share is probably a safer range to aim for.

INCREASE IN CASH DIVIDEND POSSIBLE. Studies [2] have shown, that if the dividend is *not* increased when the stock is split, the stock's adjusted price may decrease rather than increase. This has held true even when the entire market is advancing and is contrary to accepted public opinion that a split stock will automatically sell at a higher adjusted price. Companies that have accompanied stock splits with increases in the cash dividend have experienced a much better stock price reaction than companies that split without increasing the dividend.

EARNINGS TREND UP. Earnings should be on the increase when a stock is split. A stock split usually indicates that management believes the company has achieved a certain earnings

---

[1] See page 27.
[2] For example, see C. Austin Barker, "Stock Splits in a Bull Market," *Harvard Business Review*, May-June 1957, pp. 72–79.

base from which earnings are expected to go higher. If earnings are expected to decline, a stock split generally would be inappropriate, since lower earnings usually result in a lower stock price, and a split may reduce the stock to too low a level. An exception to this rule might be made, however, if a stock is selling at an exceptionally high price or has an exceptionally thin market.

ENDING OF FISCAL YEAR. One of the complications of a stock split is that adjustments must always be made in all figures that are based on the number of shares outstanding. These include, among others, per-share earnings, dividends per share, equity per share, and historical price range of the stock. The company must adjust such figures for prior years to make comparisons meaningful. Therefore, it is helpful to split a stock towards the end of the year. In that way, the forthcoming annual report can be based on the new figures and can include statistical material that is adjusted for the split. If the split occurs after the report is printed, it means that for the remainder of the period the information included in the annual report will have to be adjusted each time per-share figures are referred to.

Determining Size of Split. The company should first determine the price at which it would like the split stock to sell. Then it should determine the lowest level at which the split stock might realistically sell if it were to decline in price for no specific reason other than normal fluctuations. Such planning will help management to decide whether the desired price is too low. If it is, the split will have to be made smaller.

A company with a cyclical business should keep in mind that earnings may be substantially lower at the bottom of the business cycle and that the price of the stock may go far below the level at which management would like to see it. Companies must realistically appraise future earnings and try to interpret their effect on the price of the stock. The size of the stock split should take into consideration the price the stock will sell for under foreseeable circumstances. To find a realistic price at which a stock might sell, the following should be considered: price range of stock in preceeding six to twelve months, future earnings outlook, cyclical nature of company's business, and approximate stage of business and stock market cycles.

Pitfalls of Stock Splitting.   The major pitfall in splitting a stock is that the price may drop much lower than was anticipated when the action was taken. To avoid this, a stock price should be thought of in terms of a range rather than as a specific figure. The best precaution: Translate a stock's present range to its post-split range. Suppose a stock sold at $40 before a split, but had a range in the preceeding 12 months of $35 to $45 a share. If it had a similar range following a two-for-one split, the stock would fluctuate between $17.50 and $22.50. If a company's business is cyclical, and its stock is split at the height of a business cycle, the stock could sell well below $17.50 per share in a less favorable environment. Or the price may drop because of a general decline in the stock market, a reappraisal of the industry the company is in, a reassessment of the company's future, or an actual decline in earnings.

While it is advisable to split a stock to have it sell at lower levels, there is a point below which a low price ceases to be an advantage and may actually become a hindrance. The attitudes of the financial community towards low-priced stocks may be summed up as follows:

1. *Investors:* Many investors equate the selling price of a company's stock with quality. Low-priced stocks have unfavorable connotations, being usually thought of as highly speculative, and can result in companies developing a stockholder list composed of speculators with a rapid turnover rather than of long-term investors.

2. *Brokerage firms:* A number of brokerage firms make it a policy never to recommend formally a stock selling for less than $10. Some set an unofficial limit even higher. If a company's stock falls below such a level, it automatically is excluded from being recommended by some of the largest firms in the country.

3. *Institutional investors:* Institutional investors, such as mutual funds, rarely buy stocks that are selling at a low price. They do not like their published portfolios to indicate that they are dabbling in low-priced, presumably speculative issues.

4. *Credit institutions:* Investors who use their securities as collateral for loans will find that many banks will not accept a stock selling for less than $10 as security. This means that stockholders who normally use stocks as collateral will have to invest in other securities.

When Not To Split. There are times when a company should consider postponing a stock split. The red flags that warn to "think twice" before splitting have been detailed by the New York Stock Exchange in a guide issued for company management:

. . . the Exchange takes the position that a split-up is not in the public interest in the case of a company which, because of the nature of its business, its capitalization, or other factors, has a record of widely fluctuating earnings with alternating years of substantial profits and heavy losses. The Exchange will weigh these factors carefully when considering authorization of the listing of additional shares resulting from a split-up proposed immediately after a substantial and rapid rise in market price without any record of the stock having consistently maintained such higher price range. A split-up of a stock already selling in a low price range, and a split-up which may result in an abnormally low price range for the split-up shares, also will be carefully scrutinized.

In view of the number and variety of factors to be considered in each case, it is not practicable to fix any formula for determination of the market price at which a split-up becomes desirable, nor the ratio appropriate for a split-up. As to the latter, however, the Exchange's studies tend to indicate that, as a general matter, the most favorable price level for listed stocks is in the range of 18 to 25.[3]

"Side Effects" of Splitting. Once a company has decided to split its stock, it should be aware of a few "side effects" attendant on stock splitting. Such considerations are presented for background information. They are not factors that should determine the value of a stock split.

When a company splits its stock, its future stockholders pay proportionately higher commissions to buy or sell the same dollar amounts of stock. Such is the case because the

---

[3] New York Stock Exchange, *Company Manual.* Reprinted by permission.

cost of buying a certain dollar amount of stock goes up as the per-share price of the stock goes down. For example, when an investor purchases securities worth $4,000, the total commission he pays depends on the price of the stock. If he buys 100 shares of a stock selling at $40 per share, he pays $39 in commissions. If his $4,000 is to buy 200 shares of a stock selling at $20 per share, he pays $27 in commissions for each 100 shares, or a total of $54 in commissions. Thus, the $20 stock cost the investor an additional $15—or 38 per cent—more in commissions than the $40 stock although value of the investor's purchase was constant.

Stock-splitting will also cost the company more money. First, since more shares are outstanding as a result of the split, a company will have higher transfer costs. Second—since there presumably will be more stockholders—more quarterly reports, more welcoming letters, and more annual reports, to name just a few of the many publications, will have to be mailed. Such printing and mailing costs will increase stockholder-relations expenses.

3

Convertible Securities and Preemptive Rights

There are many ways for a corporation to finance its capital requirements. In addition to generating its funds internally, it may choose to issue common stock or preferred stock, or to use some form of short- or long-term debt.

The method that a company selects will directly influence, among many other things, its total earnings, per-share results, dividend policy, ability to raise additional capital, and growth rate—all of which will be reflected in the price of the company's common stock.

For example, American Telephone and Telegraph Company has financed its growth by keeping its debt ratio between 30% and 40%, while many independent telephone companies have not hesitated to have debt ratios as high as 60 per cent. If A.T.&T. had not deliberately chosen such a conservative debt policy, but had used a 60 per cent debt ratio, its per share earnings would have been remarkably higher than those it actually reported and its year-to-year earnings increases would have placed it in the category of a true growth stock. The A.T.&T. stockholder would undoubtedly have his stock selling at a much higher price than it is today.

The reasons for using various techniques of financing have been amply discussed in finance books and are widely understood in the financial community. However, there are two methods of raising capital that need further amplification within the context of investor relations. Both methods have an immediate effect on the company's relationship with its stockholders. One involves financing with convertible securities; the other, using preemptive rights.

This chapter shows how through planning and control a company may reap the greatest benefits of convertible-bond financing while reducing the impact of earnings dilution. It also explains the dangers—mostly unrecognized—in financing through preemptive rights and why they are not necessarily the best way to obtain new capital despite stockholders' affection for them.

CONVERTIBLE SECURITIES

Convertible securities can be an important and flexible instrument in a company's capitalization. They can be used in connection with acquisitions, when the market for the sale of new common stock is poor, when it is important to defer equity dilution, when large sums must be raised, and when an inexpensive means of raising additional capital seems appropriate.

Advantages. Among the reasons that make convertibles such an important management tool for obtaining capital efficiently are the following:

REDUCTION OF EARNINGS DILUTION. Convertible securities delay the increase in the number of shares outstanding so that earnings can advance before dilution occurs. The reverse is true in common-stock financing. For example, if a company sold common stock to raise $5 million to build and equip a new plant, the number of shares outstanding would be increased—and per share earnings consequently reduced—long before the plant was in operation and contributing to profits. On the other hand, if the company raised the necessary capital through the sale of convertible debentures, there would be no effect on per-share earnings—except for the relatively minor interest costs involved (see below)—until after the debentures were converted. Typically, this would occur after the new plant was contributing to earnings. However, it should be noted that corporations must report earnings both on the number of shares that would be outstanding assuming all potential dilution had occurred, and as well on shares actually outstanding.

EASE OF SALE. A convertible bond issue is usually easier to sell than a comparable common-stock offering, and often larger amounts of capital can be thus obtained. This is due to a great demand for convertibles because of the many advantages—such as protection of capital with equity participation —they offer to investors and because there is a relative scarcity of convertible securities.

FINANCING AT LOWER COST. Convertible debentures can be a relatively low cost method of raising additional capital. A lower rate of interest can be placed on convertible debentures than on straight debentures. The actual cash outlay for interest is often less than the dividend requirement for an equivalent amount of common stock because interest payments are tax deductible, dividends are not.

STOCK SALES AT PREMIUM. Through the use of convertibles, the company can, in effect, sell common stock at a price that is higher than its market value. This can be done because the attractiveness of a convertible, to an investor, usually enables a company to set the debenture conversion price at a premium over the then market price of the stock. This is in contrast to an offering of common stock which generally must be sold at a discount from its market price.

Controlling Dilution.   When a convertible bond indenture provision is drawn, it must be done in such a way that the company maintains the maximum control over the amount and timing of dilution. Otherwise, dilution will be governed by the automatic functioning of mechanical provisions rather than executive judgment. The following are four problem areas that affect per-share earnings unless specific steps to control them are taken in advance:

CALL PROVISIONS.   A company must retain the right to call either part of the issue, or the whole issue, at any time. This allows management to decide how many bonds it will call and when. If this option is not available, the company may some-day be forced to call the entire issue. Such an action will concentrate the earnings dilution in one year. Thus, if a company's earnings have been growing over the past several years at 12% a year, the growth pattern will be broken if the company creates a per share earnings dilution of more than 12% in any one year.

CONVERSION FEATURES.   Frequently there are provisions in convertible-bond financing that allow the company to increase the conversion price a few years after the financing. The purpose of increasing the conversion price is to allow the company to sell its common stock at *higher* prices as the company grows in value. On paper, the increase seems logical. But in practice the raising of the conversion price can work to the company's disadvantage.

Assuming that the company grows as expected, the common stock's price should go up. Such a price increase for the common will force all bondholders to convert their debentures *before* the conversion rate changes. If they do not, they will sustain a financial loss the day the new conversion rate becomes effective.

As a result, the company will be faced with high conversions in the year the conversion feature changes, bringing with it an unplanned earnings dilution.

INTEREST PAYMENT DATES. While often overlooked, such dates play an important role in convertible-bond financing. Incorrectly selected, interest payment dates may make it impossible for management to estimate per-share earnings. The problem evolves in this manner: When the stock's price rises to a point where the bond no longer sells at a premium over the conversion value, some bonds will be converted into the common via arbitrage. This occurs because the arbitrageur can make a profit whenever the bond price dips a fraction of a point below its value on a conversion basis. The arbitrageur gets his profit by buying the bond, selling short an equivalent amount of common stock, and eventually converting the bond into stock to cover his short position. Generally, the arbitrageur will not convert the bond—thus closing the transaction—until the date of interest payment so he can get the full interest on the bond.

As a result, a company may be flooded with the conversion of debentures into its common stock on any interest payment date, automatically raising the number of shares outstanding and lowering the earnings per share. It is easy to see, then, that if the payment date comes at the end of the year, the company's earlier earnings estimate may be wide of the mark.

To preclude such a situation, a company should set—whenever possible—its interest payment dates so they occur at times that give the company a healthy advance notice of the number of shares to be outstanding at the close of the quarter.

Ideally, interest payment dates on convertible debentures should be set on the first day of the company's fiscal year and the first day of the third quarter. Such a schedule of interest payments will give the company the greatest advance notice possible of the number of shares it will have outstanding at the end of its operating period.

CASH DIVIDEND PAYMENTS ON THE COMMON STOCK. When a company's earnings are increasing and its cash dividend is also growing, a point is soon reached where the bond will yield less than an equivalent amount of common stock. Thus, the bondholder may convert to get the higher payment.

Therefore, when a company raises its dividend to a level where the return is more attractive on the common stock than on the debenture, the increased dividend should be paid as soon after the start of the quarter as practical. That way a company will have as much advance notice as possible as to the increased amount of shares outstanding when making per-share earnings estimates.

Bondholder Relations.   Good stockholder relations can never be started too soon, and a company should treat its convertible bondholders as though they were stockholders. One obvious reason is that many, through the conversion of debentures, will join the stockholder ranks. There are two factors to keep in mind:

REGISTERED VS. BEARER BONDS. A company should always issue registered convertible bonds rather than bearer bonds: That way the bondholder can be personally notified when the bond is called. There can be no error. However, if bearer bonds are issued, the company's only way to notify its bond-holders of a call is through public media with the hope that either the bondholder, his broker, or his banker will see the call notice. If the holder of a bearer bond misses the call, he may lose a substantial amount of money—and his animosity will be directed to his broker or his banker *and* to the company that issued him bearer bonds.

Registered bonds have an added benefit. They allow the company to put the bondholder on the mailing list to receive annual reports, interim statements, an invitation to attend the company's annual meeting, and all other literature sent to the common stockholder.

EARLY CALLING OF BONDS. A company should not call its convertible bonds too quickly. A company that sells convertible bonds should be sensitive to an implied obligation to see that the bondholder has several years to participate in the benefits of his convertible before it is called for conversion. The bondholder should have time to allow the stock to appreciate sufficiently to exceed the premium over conversion value— which can be as much as 20% or more—that he may have paid. Not calling too soon also gives the bondholder the opportunity to enjoy the additional safety features of a bond that the company, in effect, promised when it asked him for capital. A convertible bond that is called too quickly following its issue will give the bondholder a loss amounting to the difference between conversion value and the price he paid.

If a company develops a reputation for calling its bonds quickly, it will have a more difficult time selling future convertible issues.

PREEMPTIVE RIGHTS

Preemptive rights grant a stockholder a right to buy new security issues—in a company in which he owns stock—in proportion to his ownership interest before the stock can be offered for sale to non-stockholders. Under most state statutes, stockholders automatically have preemptive rights *unless* the corporation's charter restricts or eliminates these rights. Despite such a provision in its charter, a company can still offer rights to its stockholders—if it should desire to do so. On the other hand, companies burdened with a rights requirement can seek stockholder approval for its elimination.

The need for rights grew out of the demand of owners of small corporations to maintain their proportionate ownership. Any change, obviously, in ownership of a corporation with only a few owners has an important impact on each owner's individual relationship to the corporation. But today for a publicly owned company with thousands of stockholders, there is rarely a problem of proportionate ownership.

Rights have become popular with stockholders not because of proportionate ownership but because they are considered to be a bargain—something almost for nothing. In reality, rights may prove to be an expensive "bargain" in terms of financing costs to the company. And what is expensive to the company is expensive to the company's stockholders.

Despite the fact that most stockholders given the choice would unquestionably be in favor of receiving rights, it does not necessarily follow that a company ought to abide by that preference. To judge whether or not rights offerings are the best way for any one company to raise money, it must weigh these factors: (1) why stockholders like rights; (2) the real benefits rights give the company; (3) the equally real disadvantages management must face when it issues rights; and (4) the cost of financing via rights versus all other approaches.

Why Stockholders Like Rights.   Rightly or wrongly, stockholders in general value the privilege of buying new security offerings at a discount from market price for these reasons:

1. They believe they are getting a bargain—say, a $50 stock for $42.
2. They can sell their rights to get an "extra dividend."
3. They can buy stock with rights that might otherwise be difficult to purchase because of a thin market in the stock.
4. They like to be able to buy a new class of a security—such as a convertible debenture—via rights if they believe the new security will become a "hot issue." Rights, in this regard, give them the privilege of buying without paying the premium the public would have to pay.
5. They claim it gives them the opportunity to maintain their relative position of ownership in a company. Although this is the most frequently advanced argument in favor of stock rights it is usually the least important. Stockholders of most publicly held companies, if they are concerned with maintaining their relative share ownership, could probably purchase additional securities on the open market with little difficulty.

Benefits to the Company.   Certainly to be considered by management are the following three benefits accruing to a company that offers its stockholders rights to subscribe to new security offerings:

1. *Ease of meeting frequent cash requirements:* Rights offerings may be the best way for a company to raise large amounts of cash frequently. For that reason, utilities typically offer rights.
2. *Stock appreciation:* Companies that offer rights issues may find

that stockholders consider them as additional dividends. This can favorably affect the market price of the stock so that new issues are sold at higher prices.

3. *Praise from critics:* Since professional stockholders consider rights an important prerogative, a company offering such rights often wins accolades from the professionals and also avoids verbal battles at annual meetings.

Disadvantages of Rights. Rights—along with all other methods of financing—have several disadvantages. They are:

1. Since only a certain amount of money can reasonably be raised from present stockholders, a rights offering that "reaches" beyond that maximum potential is subject to failure.
2. Offering rights may establish a precedent that ultimately becomes difficult to break because the stockholders have come to expect them.
3. Instead of broadening ownership, rights put more shares into the hands of many of the *same* stockholders on the books before the offering. In fact, the more successful the rights offering, the more current stockholders will acquire additional shares. And that means fewer names will be added to the stockholder list.
4. To make a rights offering effective, a discount from the current market price must be offered. That discount automatically gives an independent value to the rights themselves. Therefore, a decline in the price of the company's stock while the rights offering is in effect may wipe out—or greatly lessen— the value of the rights. Stockholders have been known to feel cheated when that happens. In addition, stockholders who through ignorance fail to sell or to exercise their rights later awaken to their error and they also feel cheated.
5. A rights offering may kill a company's otherwise glowing growth rate, which in turn can lower the price-earnings multiple at which the stock sells. To raise a specific sum, more shares have to be offered via a rights offering than via a public offering of stock. The reasons hinge on the fact that rights allow the stockholder to buy the stock at a below-market price. Therefore, rights offerings automatically put more shares in the hands of stockholders, automatically reduce per-share earnings.

Costs. If financing—irrespective of the method—is expensive to the company, then that financing will be expensive to the shareowners as well. So, when management is about to finance new capital it should weigh the relative costs of all methods. To select rights when a public offering might be less expensive would be a violation of stockholder trust. Most stockholders have insufficient background to determine the method of financing that might work out to their own best interest. Stockholder preference for preemptive offerings should naturally be taken into consideration, but it should only be one aspect in weighing the advantages and disadvantages of how a future security offering should be handled. When rights are no more expensive than the cheapest other method of financing, stockholder preference for rights may then logically tip the scales in their favor.

4

Repurchasing
Corporate Stock

Scores of companies each year, for a multitude of reasons, find themselves top-heavy with cash—literally with more money than they can prudently utilize. Martin Marietta Corporation, for example, found itself faced with surplus funds as a result of a Federal Trade Commission divestiture order that forced the company to sell some of its divisions. The excess money had, in effect, been forced on the company. This, of course, is an extreme case. The problem of excess cash is more likely to occur because of high profits and fast depreciation schedules. Many corporations find that they are able to finance their capital requirements from retained earnings and depreciation, pay an adequate dividend, and still have extra cash remaining.

Whenever a company has more cash than can be profitably employed in the business, it can solve its problem in one of two ways; return the excess capital to its stockholders through high cash dividend payments or use the extra money to repurchase its own shares.

Since an outright return of capital through large dividends presents income-tax problems for the stockholder, purchase of the company's own shares is often the most favored solution for eliminating unneeded cash.

Stock repurchasing was the solution arrived at by Martin Marietta—an offer to buy back 2 million shares of its more than 21 million shares outstanding. Many companies use stock repurchasing as the logical and expedient solution for reducing or eliminating their excess cash.

The most important effect of repurchasing stock is that earnings *per share* automatically increase because there are now fewer shares among which to distribute the amount of total earnings.

The practice of repurchasing one's own corporate stock is no longer rare within the financial community. In recent years, industrial companies have spent more money to repurchase their own shares than they have raised by selling new stock to the public. And each year these repurchasing totals grow larger than the year before. In one year, companies listed on the New York Stock Exchange spent almost $2 billion to buy back their common stock.[1] This amount substantially exceeded the purchases made that same year by mutual funds of shares listed on the New York Stock Exchange.

REPURCHASING POLICIES

Once stock repurchasing has been decided upon, management must then settle on one of two broad stock-purchasing policies:

1. Stock repurchasing designed to completely retire outstanding securities of a company with no foreseeable need for its extra cash
2. Stock repurchasing designed to reduce the possibility of future dilution of earnings caused by employee benefit plans, convertible securities, and acquisitions

[1] Leo A. Guthart, "Why Companies Are Buying Back Their Own Stock," *Financial Analysts Journal,* March-April 1967, pp. 105–110.

Repurchasing To Retire.   When a company finds it has more cash than it can employ profitably in the foreseeable future, the company can adjust its capitalization and permanently retire some of its stock through repurchases. The retiring of stock also can be used when a company is faced with a shrinkage in the size of its business. Even under such adverse conditions, a company can in this way bolster its per share results.

Paramount Pictures Corporation provided an example in this regard: From the time of its reorganization in 1949, Paramount reduced its outstanding capitalization from 3,263,276 shares to 1,670,281 shares. Even though net income more than ten years later was only 9% larger than it had been at the time of its reorganization, earnings per share rose 58%. Another benefit that retiring stock brought to Paramount was a substantial saving in its dividend payments.

Repurchasing to Avoid Dilution.   There are many occasions when a company must issue stock. Each time it does, earnings per share are automatically reduced. To guard against such dilution, companies frequently repurchase their own shares, sometimes on a planned, systematic basis.

The demands on a company to issue additional shares are clearly visible in the following routine corporate activities:

1. *Establishment of executive and employee benefits:* Fringe benefits for executives and employees are becoming more common-stock oriented every year; the various forms include stock options, bonuses, incentive compensations, profit sharing, and stock purchase programs.

2. *Issuing convertible securities and warrants:* Convertible bonds, convertible preferreds, and warrants in a corporation's capitalization represent potential demands on additional shares of common stock.

3. *Acquisition of—or mergers with—other companies:* The selling company typically prefers to be acquired for *stock*, not cash—mainly because of income-tax considerations.

4. *Stock dividends:* Obviously, any stock dividend means additional shares will be issued and outstanding.

Securities Other than Common Stock.   A company with other securities outstanding, in addition to common stock, might consider repurchasing these securities. An example would be a preferred stock, particularly one with a high dividend requirement. The reason for repurchase would be even more compelling if the preferred were convertible into common stock.

The same might be true in the case of a warrant that was selling at a comparatively low premium. Repurchase of the warrant can eliminate a potential dilution problem with a minor outlay.

PROCEDURE IN REPURCHASES

Once a company decides to embark on a program to repurchase its own stock, there are several methods open to management. Which is the best method of acquiring one's own stock will depend on the number of shares available and the speed with which the company wants to acquire its stock.

Buying on the Open Market.   The amount of stock that can be purchased in this way and the length of time required will depend on the trading volume of the issue, unless a large seller can be located.

Negotiated Purchase.   This is a good way for a company to acquire a relatively large block of its stock. The blocks are purchased from a major stockholder, the estate of a large shareowner, or an institution such as a mutual fund.

Hat Corporation of America, for example, bought 40,000 shares of its own common stock from the widow of the company's late board chairman at a negotiated price below the then current market price. Naturally, any negotiated purchase between the company and its officers, directors, or members of their families—or with any other "insider" stockholders—must be done on an arm's-length basis.

While companies look to corporate family shareowners for stock purchase possibilities, many companies ask institutions owning their shares to give them the first opportunity to buy their own stock whenever the institution decides to sell. Frequently, the institution takes the company up on the suggestion. If the company and the institution are dealing directly, commissions can be eliminated, a saving to both buyer and seller.

A negotiated purchase offers other benefits to both the company buying and the stockholder selling. Most important of these benefits is that a large amount of stock can be traded swiftly and the market price is not disrupted by a large buyer or seller.

Tender Offer.   Offering to buy shares from all stockholders has become a popular way to acquire sizeable amounts of stock at one time. A tender offer is an offer that the company makes to its stockholders to purchase a specific number of its shares by a certain date and at a stated price—the price generally being above the then current market price.

Most tender offers are made to accumulate stock from the general public. Occasionally, however, there is yet another purpose: giving a large stockholder the opportunity to sell a block of stock. For example, when Whirlpool Corporation offered to acquire 1 million shares of its stock, the largest amount, 992,000 shares, was acquired from Radio Corporation of America. Similarly, Midland-Ross Corporation asked for tenders of 225,000 shares of its stock. Midland-Ross bought all the 196,000 shares that were tendered, including almost 153,000 from M. A. Hanna Company.

Exchange of Investment Securities.   A company that owns securities of another corporation can offer these securities to its stockholders in exchange for its own stock. Eastern Gas and Fuel Associates acquired more than 1 million shares of its stock from its stockholders in exchange for the Norfolk & Western Railway Company stock that it owned. Eastern Gas stockholders received nine-tenths of a share for each Eastern Gas preferred share tendered and half a Norfolk & Western share for each share of common stock tendered.

TIMING REPURCHASES

The reason a company wants to repurchase its stock provides the chief answer to the timing question.

Regular Repurchases.   For example, if a company wants its stock for pension plans, stock options, employee purchase plans —in effect, for recurring needs—then it can repurchase its stock on a fairly consistent basis. Such regular purchases will allow management to fulfill its requirements in a way that will have little influence on the stock's market price. Furthermore, the company buying its own shares consistently will be able to dollar-average on its purchases and need not be concerned about the price paid for the shares on any individual transaction.

Anticipating Special Needs.   On the other hand, if a company wishes to repurchase stock for an acquisition, then management may have to accumulate stock over a relatively short period. Some companies attempt to anticipate acquisitions and start to repurchase their stock in advance of a specific need. By purchasing shares on the open market and then re-issuing them for an acquisition, a company gains the benefit of the earnings of the acquired company without increasing the number of shares outstanding.

The need to issue additional shares as a result of the conversion of other securities into common stock can usually be anticipated and purchases timed accordingly.

Permanent Retirement of Stock.   For the management that wishes to permanently retire its stock—thereby reducing the company's capitalization—a mechanical formula is a good way to solve the timing question. Under such a formula plan, management may set a policy that says: Repurchase whenever the stock sells below its book value, or whenever the stock is at a specific percentage below its book value, or whenever the stock sells below a predetermined price. Such plans allow for automatic repurchase on a continuing basis.

Other Factors. Two other factors that may influence management's timing are (1) a substantial decline in the price of the company's stock which makes the purchase comparatively inexpensive and (2) the sudden offering of a large block of the company's stock by a major stockholder or institution—particularly when a company's top executives can see a later use for such repurchased shares. If it is known that there is a future use for the stock it will usually be better to purchase the block when it is offered, rather than attempt the accumulation at a future, more convenient date.

LEGAL AND REGULATORY CONSIDERATIONS

There are certain legal and regulatory requirements that must be met before management can launch a stock repurchasing program. The legal considerations facing any company wishing to repurchase its shares may be reduced to two broad categories. First, there are the technical considerations that have been set up by the state in which the company is incorporated, the company's charter or its by-laws, and the company's loan agreements or indentures which may or may not restrict repurchasing.

In this technical area, the following are typical questions management and its legal counsel will need to answer: Does a state law require stockholder approval or notification before the repurchasing program may start? May purchases be made only from retained earnings? Does the company's charter allow such repurchasing? If the charter allows repurchasing, what procedure must be followed? What does the stock exchange require—assuming the company is a listed one?

Then, possible transgressions against Securities and Exchange Commission rules must be considered. For example, the Securities and Exchange Act does not permit a company to buy its own stock in order to raise or lower the price or to get others to buy or sell. Repurchasing is also not permitted when a company is engaged in or about to engage in some form of stock distribution. To illustrate, a company has to stop repurchasing its stock when it actually opens negotiations for an acquisition that would involve issuing shares.

ETHICAL CONSIDERATIONS

There are certain ethical considerations that cannot be overlooked when deciding whether or not to buy back company stock. Underlying them is the principle that repurchases must never be used as an instrument to deceive investors.

Since the amount of stock repurchased can be a determining factor in per-share earnings results, a company with a relatively flat earnings record and large cash surplus could use this device to increase per-share earnings each year. Similarly, a company with an unblemished growth record could repurchase stock if its string of consecutive earnings increases were jeopardized. Repurchases solely for these reasons could be construed as financial manipulations and should be avoided.

Stock repurchases based on favorable insider knowledge are highly unethical. All stockholders are not being treated equitably if some are selling to a buyer that is privy to relevant information not available to them. Management cannot assume that it has no obligation to a stockholder who is willing to sell his stock. The stockholder might not have sold at the offered price if he had been made aware of pertinent developments.

5

Listing on Major, Regional, and Foreign Exchanges

Listing on the New York Stock Exchange is not always a wise move. The mere fact that a company meets the minimum requirements of the Big Board does not mean that most of the benefits that are supposed to accrue from listing will actually occur. Quite the contrary. If a company lists prematurely, it only magnifies the problems it sought to overcome by listing. On the other hand, for a company that is ready for the Big Board, a New York Stock Exchange listing has many advantages.

From the time a company meets the minimum requirements for listing on the New York Stock Exchange until it actually makes its application it will be continuously faced with the problem of whether or not to take this step. Pressure to list from some stockholders and some members of the professional investment community will always place a qualified over-the-counter company in the position where it must regularly review the advisability of being traded on the New York Stock Exchange. To a lesser extent, the same situation holds true for listing on the smaller stock exchanges.

For all practical purposes, listing on the N.Y.S.E. is an irreversible step, since it is almost impossible to delist voluntarily. Because few corporate decisions are so irrevocable, a company should carefully weigh the advantages and disadvantages before taking this action.

The desirability of listing must be determined in light of each company's individual situation and objectives. To put listing in its proper perspective, the following considerations will be discussed:

1. How a company can best tell when it is ready to list
2. The benefits a company will get from a New York Stock Exchange listing, once it is prepared to list
3. The difficulties an unprepared company will encounter once listed
4. How to develop investor interest in the company after listing

DETERMINING WHEN A COMPANY IS READY TO LIST

Listed stocks act best when they have achieved broad ownership and widespread investor interest. A company with only 1,700 round-lot stockholders—the New York Stock Exchange minimum—hardly can be classified as having broad ownership. (See Fig. 5–1 for New York Stock Exchange minimum requirements.) The minimum requirements are even less stringent for listing on exchanges other than the New York Stock Exchange. For example, to list on the American Stock Exchange, a company need have only 250,000 shares in public hands, as opposed to 700,000 on the Big Board, with a minimum value of $1,250,-000—not the $12 million demanded by the New York Stock Exchange. Obviously, then, *if a company sees danger in listing on the New York Stock Exchange when it barely meets Big Board criteria, it can expect even poorer results if it lists on another exchange merely because of more lenient standards.*

Number of stockholders

Total 2,000
Holders of 100 shares or more 1,700
  (The number of beneficial holders of stock held in the name of NYSE member organizations will be considered in addition to holders of record)

Number of shares

Total outstanding 1,000,000
Publicly held 700,000

Market value publicly-held shares $12,000,000
  (Net tangible assets should be $10,000,000 although greater emphasis is placed on market value)

Demonstrated earning power under competitive conditions (normally for at least 3 years)

Pre-tax $2,000,000
Net income $1,200,000

Fig. 5–1. Minimum Numerical Standards of Eligibility for Listing on New York Stock Exchange.

A listed stock must be able to generate its own market and be able to compete with other listed securities for public investor interest. A company should first prove its ability to attract widespread trading interest in its stock in the over-the-counter market. Otherwise, that stock is unlikely to enjoy any better success in a listed market where there is no sponsorship by over-the-counter firms.

In determining whether a company's stock is performing well enough in the over-the-counter market to anticipate a successful listed performance, the following criteria should be met:

1. About 10 good firms should be making primary markets in the stock.
2. There should be a narrow range between the bid and asked price—i.e., a half-point spread in a stock selling at between $20 and $40, an even smaller one in a stock selling below $20.
3. The trading volume, as far as can be determined from the transfer sheets, should average close to 1,000 shares a day.
4. The total number of stockholders should be more than *double* the 1,700 round-lot holders required by the New York Stock Exchange.

ADVANTAGES OF LISTING

Among the many benefits that come with a listing on the New York Stock Exchange—*when a company is ready for listing*—are the following:

1. *Prestige:* There is no question that it is more prestigious for a company to be listed on the New York Stock Exchange than to be traded in the over-the-counter market. Generally, the smaller the company the greater the increase in prestige it will gain by being listed.

2. *New stockholders:* There are many individuals who purchase only listed stocks. Thus, companies that list, instantly expand the number of potential investors. New stockholders who are attracted to the company usually supplement rather than replace the number of existing stockholders. As a result, a company often achieves a net gain in the number of its stockholders by listing.

3. *Increased institutional ownership:* Institutions overwhelmingly prefer listed stocks. The portfolio of a mutual fund, for example, is an important selling tool for salesmen. Having a large portion of its investments in securities listed on the New York Stock Exchange enables it to attract more holders to its fund. Even when their portfolios are not published, many institutions prefer to own listed stocks. Savings banks in New York and other states are limited by law to listed common stocks for their portfolios.

4. *Broker interest:* Many brokerage firms prefer to recommend N.Y.S.E.-listed stocks simply because there is greater acceptance by their customers of such recommendations—which, in turn, enables the brokers to generate increased business.

5. *Increased volume:* Increased investment interest, which may come with listing on the New York Stock Exchange, can result in greater trading volume of a company's securities.

6. *Greater market stability:* Increased trading volume will help to narrow the spread in the stock's bid and asked prices. This will allow a greater number of shares to be bought and sold without wide fluctuations in the stock's price. Furthermore,

the New York Stock Exchange specialist handling the listed security also acts to narrow the spread between bid and asked prices.

7. *Acquisitions facilitated:* Big Board listing can make acquisitions through an exchange of stock easier because some businessmen incorrectly equate a listed stock with financial solidity and instant liquidity.

In addition, an over-the-counter company that intended to keep that status would have great difficulty acquiring a listed company. Most stockholders of a company listed on the New York Stock Exchange would rebel at the idea of being acquired by an over-the-counter company—no matter how large the over-the-counter company was—if they were to receive an over-the-counter stock in exchange for their listed one.

8. *Higher price-earnings ratios:* The Bank of New York, in a study of common stock prices, concluded that stocks listed on the New York Stock Exchange sell at higher price-earnings multiples than do over-the-counter stocks. According to the Bank of New York, a New York Stock Exchange stock commands—on average—a price-earnings ratio three multiples higher than that of an issue with similar characteristics traded over-the-counter.[1]

9. *More newspapers carrying quotations:* Daily newspapers publish more complete quotations of listed stocks than they do of over-the-counter stocks. Of the listed stocks quoted, those on the New York Stock Exchange are most widely quoted in the newspapers. Listing makes it easy for stockholders and potential stockholders to follow daily price changes.

DRAWBACKS TO LISTING

Listing contains some serious pitfalls if a company lists *before* it is ready. When this happens, many of the advantages of listing may boomerang.

Decline in Investment Interest. Many brokerage firms—even members of the New York Stock Exchange—that previously

[1] Speech by Manown Kisor, Jr., "The Bank of New York Common Stock Valuation Study," May 7, 1964.

traded a company's stock in the over-the-counter market will no longer have an interest in the company once it lists. This withdrawal of support, if not adequately replaced, can seriously undermine the investment position of a company. In discussing how support is generated for a company's stock by over-the-counter dealers, New York Stock Exchange President Robert W. Haack, then president of the National Association of Securities Dealers, Inc., said:

By far, the most important advantage of the OTC market is . . . dealer support and sponsorship. Prior to the development of a broad and spontaneous market for its stock, a company is dependent upon the over-the-counter dealer for the maintenance of a primary market and stimulation of investor interest. The activities of dealers are determined both by investment attraction of the stock and the profitability of trading and distributing the issue. Consequently, exchange listing which eliminates the dealer market, will definitely result in loss of interest by non-members of the exchange and possibly even a reduction of interest for dealers who are exchange members. This is evidenced by the fact that just prior to the opening of trading of a newly listed stock on a stock exchange, most of the primary market makers sell their long position or cover their short position and go on to other merchandise.

Interest in a stock is generated in many ways. A company with an outstanding new process or product may find itself bathed in publicity from inception. A good example of this is Comsat. On the other hand, many an outstanding, profitable company in a long-established industry may go unnoticed for years. The majority of small, publicly-owned companies are similarly unspectacular. They do not attract the attention of the public and, therefore, remain uninviting to investors unless some effort is made to draw the stock to the public's attention. The initial distribution of an issue for such a company, the maintenance of this activity as well as subsequent high interest levels is the primary concern of the OTC market maker . . .

While listing a security may to some extent stimulate a sudden investor interest through attending publicity, such would be the case only where there is this broad and spontaneous market to begin with, so that the impact of listing more than offsets the loss of dealer support and merchandising.

In the over-the-counter securities business, the primary market maker accepts the responsibility for maintaining a fair and orderly market and in helping a company broaden investor interest in its securities. This responsibility to provide the best possible market for a stock is not just theoretical, since the primary market maker will generally have substantial capital committed in maintaining his inventory. Primary market makers can also be of great help to a company and the market for its stock in many other ways; such as advising the company on matters of financial policy, financial public relations, financial reporting, dissemination of reports and supplying current information to members of the financial and investing community. All of these activities are designed to stimulate interest in a company and its securities on the part of other broker/dealers and potential investors.

In many cases, the combined capital available for investment in a security by primary market makers far exceeds the capital resources of the specialist who might trade the security of an exchange. Such primary market makers have a beneficial effect on supply and demand through their merchandising activities and through contact with investors. On the other hand, the exchange specialist must rely largely on the spontaneous flow of buy and sell orders in the market place and thus has limited capacity to cope with periodic imbalances in this relationship.[2]

Decline in Trading Volume. There have been many instances where the trading volume in a newly listed company deteriorated without the support of over-the-counter dealers interested in maintaining markets and finding buyers and sellers.

Although the New York Stock Exchange reports a mammoth trading volume each year, a relatively small number of companies account for most of this volume. The majority of companies listed on the Big Board have limited trading activity. For example, a study by Rockwell Manufacturing Company indicates that the annual volume of trading in Rockwell's stock in the over-the-counter market was greater than that of 75% of the companies listed on the New York Stock Exchange and greater than 93% of the companies on the American Stock Exchange in the year of the study.

Decline in Price. Listing is not a guarantee for continuing upward prices for the company's stock. Far from it. In a study of 42 over-the-counter stocks that listed on the New York Stock Exchange, some 28 of those stocks had declined in listing price two years later. This action was contrary to that experienced by the 35 stocks comprising the National Quotations Bureau index of over-the-counter stocks during the same time span.

GENERATING INVESTMENT INTEREST AFTER LISTING

No matter how well a company meets all qualifications for listing, the transition period—which can last from one month to

[2] Robert W. Haack, "Advantages of the Over-the-Counter Market," address to American Management Association Seminar, February 19, 1965.

several years after listing—can be a difficult time during which the stock's price and trading volume may decline. One reason for this reaction is that a company often changes its status; rather than being one of the larger over-the-counter companies it becomes one of the smaller New York Stock Exchange companies. As a consequence its following may change from a number of active broker-dealer firms to a smaller—and probably less enthusiastic—audience of brokerage houses. To make the transition as smooth as possible, a company should develop a program to generate increased interest in itself on the part of the financial community. Among the ways a company can accomplish the task of building interest are the following.

Security Analyst Meetings.   Meetings should be scheduled with more than normal frequency immediately after listing (see Chapter 10). They should be held in all the important financial centers, such as Boston, Philadelphia, San Francisco, Los Angeles, and Chicago, as well as in New York. This is also one of the best times to schedule talks before regional security analyst societies.

In addition, a company should change the composition of its meetings. Analysts from firms that have previously been following the company may no longer have an interest once the stock is listed. Other analysts will find the company of interest only because the listing has taken place.

News Announcements and Feature Stories.   Whenever announcements of company events can be controlled they should be timed to occur during the transitional period so that the company will get favorable attention in the financial press. Typical of beneficial announcements are those of a major new product, a large plant expansion, or a favorable earnings projection.

Although it is difficult to have feature articles about a company appear on a schedule, there are some ways in which management can accomplish this. For example, interviews with interested publications can be timed so that articles will appear shortly after the listing.

Internal Corporate Actions.   A dividend increase shortly after listing is one of the ways to focus attention on a company.

Mailings to Stockholders. Stockholders should receive a letter announcing the listing. They should also receive additional communications from the company in connection with other parts of the "transition program," such as a reprint of a talk before a security analyst group.

DUAL LISTING ON REGIONAL EXCHANGES

Once a company has listed on a major New York exchange, it is still faced with the decision of whether or not to list on a regional stock exchange. The advantages to be obtained from a regional listing differ somewhat from those obtained via a New York Stock Exchange listing. However, regional exchanges perform specialized functions that can create increased market interest and broadened stock ownership.

As general rule, it is only the large companies with actively traded stocks and with stockholders numbering in the tens of thousands that can benefit from the additional listings.

Dual listing—listing on a regional exchange as well as on a New York exchange—can increase the marketability, public and professional interest, and distribution of a company's securities. Better than half of the common stocks listed in the New York Stock Exchange also are traded on one or more regional exchanges. About 80 per cent of the dollar volume of transactions occurring on regional stock exchanges—such as the Boston, Detroit, Honolulu, Midwest, Pacific Coast, and Philadelphia-Baltimore Stock Exchanges—is in dually traded securities.

The popularity of dual listing, however, does not mean that any company now listed on the New York Stock Exchange should automatically apply for regional listing. In fact, most companies that are listed on the Big Board have no need for a dual listing.

To list on another exchange, a company must first be actively traded on the New York Stock Exchange. A company whose stock is *not* actively traded on the Big Board will find that the number of transactions in its stock on a regional exchange will be extremely limited. A regional listing is no guarantee that any trading activity of consequence will take place there.

The Midwest Stock Exchange suggests that a company should have at least 3 million shares outstanding and about 10,000 stockholders to get real benefit from a dual listing. Naturally, such rules of thumb are subject to individual exceptions.

Advantages. The advantages of dual listing may be summarized as follows:

TRADING CONTINUES FOR LONGER PERIODS. The New York Stock Exchange's trading day *ends* at 12:30 p.m. on the Pacific Coast, at 10:30 a.m. in Hawaii. Since regional exchanges operate on local time, any New York Stock Exchange stock that is listed on a regional exchange in a time zone other than the Eastern time zone gets the benefit of being traded for at least one hour—in other cases several hours—after the market closes in New York. Security brokers in the Midwest and on the West Coast take a greater interest in and are more likely to recommend stock that can be bought and sold during the entire course of their working day.

IMPROVED MARKET. Listing on a regional stock exchange can improve the market being made for a stock on the New York exchange. For example, a Securities and Exchange Commission study found that after the Midwest Exchange developed a substantial volume in Commonwealth Edison Company stock, the spread in the New York Stock Exchange specialist's bid and asked quotations showed a noticeable improvement.

GREATER AVAILABILITY OF STOCK QUOTATIONS. As a by-product of being traded on more than one exchange, a dually listed company gets better newspaper coverage in the reporting of its stock's price. Many smaller daily newspapers do not print complete tables of stocks traded on the New York and American Stock Exchanges. However, these newspapers usually include the full tabulation of stocks traded on their local regional exchange; this is the only way some stockholders can conveniently obtain quotations on the stocks they hold.

PROFESSIONAL INVESTOR INTEREST. Since a number of major regional stock exchanges allow their members to split their commissions with non-members, mutual funds—heavy buyers and sellers of common stocks—look with favor on a New York Stock Exchange stock that is dually listed. Their reason is economic.

The mutual funds, in one fashion or another, reward brokerage houses for selling their fund shares. Most of the time, such rewards are in terms of commissions. This can be done by the institution's purchase or sale of securities through the brokerage firm to be rewarded. More typically, the institution buys or sells through firms equipped to handle large-scale transactions and at the same time requires that firm to split the commissions generated with the firm to which the institution has the obligation.

However, the New York Stock Exchange does not permit its members to split commissions with non-member firms if the transaction occurred on the New York Stock Exchange. But the same firm can split commissions with a non-member firm if it executes the order on a regional exchange—other than the Midwest Stock Exchange which has a rule similar to that of the New York Stock Exchange. It works this way:

A mutual fund, for example, wants to pay a non-New York Stock Exchange brokerage house $2,000 in commissions for having sold its shares to the public. The fund decides to buy a stock that is traded on both the Big Board and the Detroit Exchange. The fund instructs a New York Stock Exchange member who also has a seat on the Detroit Exchange to buy that stock for the fund *on the Detroit Exchange* and give up—or split—a portion of its commission (say $5,000 in total commission) to the non-New York Stock Exchange firm. That way, the mutual fund's $2,000 obligation is fulfilled but the fund has not paid more than the regular commission rate.

Still another trend may lead to even greater institutional interest in companies that are listed on regional exchanges as well as on the Big Board. Some publicly owned mutual fund management companies, through subsidiaries, have been admitted to membership in the Pacific Coast Exchange—an action prohibited on the New York Stock Exchange. As a member, the fund, in effect, can buy and sell stock and save the cost of most of the commission. The savings on commissions can run into the hundreds of thousands of dollars.

Other institutions, such as pension funds or insurance companies, may follow the example of the management companies in an attempt to lower their brokerage costs. If such a development spreads, companies listed on the New York Stock Exchange may feel additional pressure to list on regional exchanges.

Disadvantages. If a company can generate adequate investor interest, the advantages of dual listing far outweigh the minor disadvantages attendant upon such a step. Yet, it is important to know what drawbacks are inherent in dual listing.

TIMING PRESS RELEASES. Dual listing makes it more difficult to release news to the press *after* the market has closed. Announcements made after the close—by a company solely listed on the New York Stock Exchange—give all investors the news when no one investor can act on the information ahead of any others. Since dual listing extends the trading day, any news announcement made after 3:30 p.m. (New York time) will still enable some investors to act on the news that day by buying or selling shares on the regional exchange.

COSTS. Listing on a regional exchange also adds to a company's expenses. To the direct cost of listing must be added the costs of record keeping, notification, and bookkeeping and the expenses of dealing with several regional transfer agents instead of only one agent.

LISTING ON A FOREIGN EXCHANGE

As American companies become more active in overseas affairs—as they attract foreign stockholders, buy into European companies, set up foreign subsidiaries, construct plants abroad, or intensify their export activities—they should consider the advantages of a foreign listing. After careful consideration, most companies will conclude that they should not yet take such a step. But a few will find good reasons to list overseas now.

The number of American companies listed on foreign stock exchanges has been growing steadily and is now in the hundreds. Despite the trend, the results that can be accomplished by such a listing are relatively limited for the United States company. At best, the benefits to be gained from a foreign listing are, in most cases, long term.

While only a relative handful of companies each year will find it necessary to even consider a foreign listing, any company should be aware of: (1) the guidelines best used to determine whether or not a company ought to list abroad, (2) the facts surrounding a foreign listing, and (3) the necessity to conduct (once listed) an investment-community relations program in Europe. The following discussion will confine itself to European stock exchanges, since they are the only foreign exchanges on which an American company will currently consider listing. Currency exchange controls, as well as other factors, have acted to block American companies—except in rare cases—from listing on exchanges in Australia, Japan, Mexico, South America, and other localities.

Guidelines for Decision to List Abroad. Companies with wide European interests are naturally the most logical ones to consider listing abroad. Any United States company with extensive manufacturing operations in Europe or whose products—especially when they are well-known consumer products—are sold widely in Europe has good reason to consider listing. Certainly, any company whose future plans call for a sales penetration of European markets or for setting up large manufacturing facilities abroad should also consider listing in anticipation of such expansion.

Other reasons for considering foreign listing include:

1. A large number of stockholders in European countries
2. An anticipated need by a company or its subsidiaries operating abroad to raise money in European markets
3. An acquisition program that involves buying foreign companies

While there are benefits to be derived from listing abroad, they do not automatically—nor even eventually—occur for every company that lists in Europe. The chief benefits that accrue to a company listing abroad are: the opening up of new sources of capital, protection against nationalistic—and sometimes hostile—actions against foreign-based firms, and a broadening of the market for its stock.

OPENING UP NEW SOURCES OF CAPITAL. As the European economy continues to prosper—and as its standard of living concurrently grows—stock ownership by Europeans will undoubtedly become more widespread, paralleling the increase in investors in this country starting with World War II. Such capital sources have already been tapped by United States companies. Using convertible bonds, General Electric Company, Pepsico, Inc., Bristol-Myers Company, Owens-Illinois, Inc., Monsanto Company and other companies have raised substantial funds by selling securities abroad.

Protection Against Nationalism. Many European government authorities and businessmen believe that their own industries are being threatened by the domination of American corporations. As a result, pressures are growing to curb the operations of American companies. Listing can encourage foreign-investor ownership which, in turn, helps create a friendlier climate in the European financial community. Encouraging ownership by foreign nationals in the parent company is another way of offsetting pressures for direct native ownership in local operations of American firms.

The European public's financial familiarity with the parent company—as a result of local stock ownership—can also be of assistance when a subsidiary wishes to do any direct financing in the country in which it operates.

Broadened Stockholder Base. Increasing the marketability of a company's securities and broadening its stockholder base will not be accomplished solely by listing on a foreign exchange. Morgan Guaranty Trust Company has concluded that, "So far foreign listing, per se, has not generally resulted in a significant broadening of ownership." [3] From an American standpoint, European markets even for local shares are relatively thin and more so for shares of United States companies. However, although a foreign listing does not automatically mean more stockholders it does give a company a better *opportunity* to increase the number of its European stockholders (see below, "Investor Relations Abroad," page 62).

It is difficult to determine the actual results of foreign listing. Volume figures are almost impossible to check since they are not reported by European exchanges in the same way as they are in the United States. It is also difficult to determine if there has been an increase in the number of European stockholders since stocks of American corporations on European exchanges are held by only a few nominees. Rarely are the stocks registered in the individual stockholder's name.

Choosing a Foreign Exchange.   When a company decides to list abroad, it must then determine on which exchange to list. The answer will depend on the company's degree of interest in each European country in terms of:

1. The number of stockholders the company has in the country
2. The extent of the company's manufacturing operations in the country
3. The number of employees in the country
4. The countries where the company's products are sold
5. The political climate—friendly or hostile towards American concerns
6. The United States firm's future plans concerning any of the above five factors

Sometimes, foreign financial institutions will request a company to apply for a listing on a specific exchange. Compliance may be appropriate to maintain the goodwill of local bankers and governmental authorities.

Costs can be a deciding point in determining which exchange is best since some exchanges are considerably more expensive

[3] Morgan Guaranty Trust Company of New York, "The Requirements for Listing and the Methods of Trading United States Securities on Foreign Stock Exchanges," November, 1965, pg. 3.

than others. The attitude of the government of a particular country towards American companies listing on its exchanges can also be important. Some countries actively encourage the listing of American companies; others have erected barriers, either regulatory or financial, which make it difficult for American firms to list. The procedure for listing on a foreign exchange usually takes anywhere from three to six months. Some exchanges require complicated applications; others require relatively simple ones.

The principal exchanges for any United States company to consider—in terms of the exchanges' importance as financial centers and the prestige factors surrounding such exchanges—are, alphabetically, as follows: Amsterdam Stock Exchange, Brussels Bourse, Frankfurt Stock Exchange, London Stock Exchange, Paris Bourse, and the Swiss Stock Exchanges.

Investor Relations Abroad. To build up European-investor interest, any United States company that lists on a foreign exchange must set up an investment-community relations program in Europe similar to its domestic program.

The foreign program must be launched with the understanding that financial reporting in the European press about American companies is comparatively meager. Language differences plus the distance factor combine to make it still more difficult for European investors and European security analysts to keep current on American companies.

TRANSLATED COMMUNICATIONS. The language-barrier problem can be partially overcome by publishing a foreign-language edition of the company reports—provided of course, the company has a large concentration of stockholders speaking a common foreign language. Some of the larger international companies publish a summary of the annual report in one or more foreign languages. American Express Company has issued separate annual reports in French, German, Italian, and Spanish. Philip Morris, Inc., has printed the president's letter in its annual report in five languages: English, French, German, Italian, and Spanish. General Motors Corporation has issued a digest of its annual report in four languages: French, German, Spanish, and Portugese.

An interesting sidelight to foreign-stockholder communications is the attitude of various nationals towards such translated reports. A survey has reported that Dutch businessmen so pride themselves on their knowledge of English that they dislike having translated reports. On the other hand, the survey indicated that the French clearly expressed a preference for reports in their own language.

TIME AND DISTANCE. Distance makes it difficult to get news into the hands of foreign stockholders while it is still fresh. The time problem is compounded by the fact that a United States company must send reports to a nominee for forwarding to the beneficial stockholder. Unfortunately, European nominees treat such material differently than do their American counterparts and do not automatically send the material along to the beneficial stockholder. As a result, American companies receive proxies from a much smaller percentage of their foreign than of their American stockholders.

THE FOREIGN FINANCIAL COMMUNITY AND THE PRESS. To help get news into the hands of the European stockholder, it is necessary for an American company to work closely with foreign banks. The company should also distribute its news announcements to foreign news services and the foreign press.

An American company that lists on a foreign exchange should be cognizant of its responsibility to European security analysts. Executives who have held meetings with financial institutions and security analysts in Europe have found a welcome reception.

FOREIGN EMPLOYEE STOCK OWNERSHIP. One way for a United States company to broaden its stockholder base is to encourage its foreign employees to become stockholders. While employee stock ownership is an accepted practice in the United States, it is relatively rare abroad. Many foreign nationals are unfamiliar with common stock although they may have some familiarity with *interest-bearing* securities. Thus, the use of convertible bonds of the parent company or of its subsidiaries for employee savings plans is one way to introduce foreign employees gradually to equity security ownership.

DEPOSITORY RECEIPTS.   To further smooth its European-investor relations, a United States company listed abroad should recognize that the stock certificate used as the basis for exchange of ownership in the United States is not a practical unit for exchange in overseas markets. A more convenient unit is the "depository receipt."

A company can arrange for United States banks and trust companies to issue, through their foreign branches and correspondents, depository receipts for United States corporate shares. The depository receipts can be divided into fractions of shares to bring the stock's selling price closer to those customary in foreign markets. The receipts can also be printed in the language of the country in which they are to be traded.

For example, when General Motors Corporation listed its common stock on the London Stock Exchange, it arranged for bearer depository receipts to be issued by Barclays Bank, Ltd. Each depository receipt unit represents one-twentieth of a full share of G.M. common stock.

6

Defending
Company Control

The managements of many publicly owned companies live in fear that they will awaken one morning to the news that an insurgent group is actively attempting to gain control of their company. The excellence of management has no real bearing on the problem. A well-managed company may be captured by tender offer, a bid by outsiders to buy a specified number of shares of the company's stock from the public at a price above the market quotation. A poorly managed company may be won by either the tender offer or by a proxy-fight, a procedure wherein an outsider tries to oust the current management by soliciting votes from the company's shareholders. Few companies are secure from such take-over attempts.

Of the two approaches, the tender offer is cleaner, faster, and often less costly than the proxy fight. For those reasons the tender offer is becoming increasingly popular. Unfortunately, it is the more difficult take-over method for management to defeat.

There are many steps a company can take to limit its potential as a victim of outside aggression, and there are also many preparations management must make to gird itself for battle should a proxy fight or tender offer suddenly appear. If the right preparations have been taken far enough in advance, management stands a good chance of defeating an outside attempt to gain control.

THE PROXY FIGHT

How To Spot a Proxy Raid Early. Each month, the percentage of stock held by each stockholder group—that is, individual stockholders, stock held in brokers' names, and stock held in nominees' names—should be tabulated. Ordinarily, there should be little month-to-month change in the percentage of stock held by each group. In fact, these holdings typically conform to a pattern—an individual pattern for each company—that management can easily recognize. Even if, in the course of several months, the percentage of stock held by individuals goes up, there is usually little reason for corporate concern unless the increase is concentrated in a few names. But, if the per cent of stock held in brokers' names or held by nominees shows an increasing trend, the stock-buying ought to be investigated.

To detect such outside accumulation of stock, knowledge of the nominee names used by banks and other institutions is necessary because banks and financial institutions use different nominee names for themselves and other beneficial owners of stock such as estates, trusts, investment management accounts, corporate trust accounts, and safekeeping and custody accounts. The "Nominee List," a publication of the American Society of Corporate Secretaries, Inc., is a useful tool in that it identifies many nominees.

Even when there are no increases in the *total* holdings of brokers or nominees, changes within those groups still occur. Therefore, each month the number of shares attributable to any large holder—individual, broker, or nominee—should be compared with a table showing the amount of stock held by every name on the list in each of the previous six months. While the number of shares in each name will normally vary from month to month, a steady accumulation will show itself readily and a pattern will become apparent.

Purchases in nominees' names usually indicate nothing more sinister than an institution such as a mutual fund or bank, establishing a normal investment position in the company. However, if an accumulation in a nominee's name that is not attributable to a recognizable source occurs, every effort should be made— through contacts in the investment community—to trace the stock purchaser.

This hard-to-get information often can be obtained through feedbacks from brokers. As a matter of good financial relations, a company should maintain regular and closer relationships with many brokerage firms. Such relationships not only serve the obvious purpose of keeping the financial community informed about the company's activities but also serve the less apparent purpose of keeping the company alerted to what the financial community is doing and thinking about the company.

Such feedback is vital if a company is to keep one step ahead of take-over maneuvers. Feedback works this way: Any group that is out to purchase control of a company attempts to conduct its initial efforts in absolute secrecy. Yet, since most purchasing of stock must be made through normal brokerage channels, an increasingly large number of people on the inside will learn about the situation. If relationships between the company and brokerage houses have been good, inside financial sources will be in a position to alert the company that a take-over is in the offing.

Targets for a Proxy Fight. The characteristics of a company that attract outsiders who look to gain control of a company are found in a company's financial portrait. The characteristics are:

1. *Large surplus cash position:* Extra cash is always an open invitation to raiders who are attracted by the opportunity to use another's funds for the launching or the enrichment of a financial empire.

2. *Stock selling substantially below book value:* In such cases, liquidation will bring a substantial profit to the stockhold-

ers since the company is literally worth more dead than alive. Such a situation will also bring big profits to a liquidator—in this case, the outsiders who wrest control from management.

3. *Understated assets:* When assets on a company's books are stated at low cost, the price of the company's stock may not reflect the real value of those assets. Companies with mineral holdings or large tracts of real estate purchased years ago may well have such assets understated, and they can be sold at their true value by an outsider group that captures control of the company.

4. *Small percentage of closely held stock:* Managements that own nominal amounts of their company's stock are in a weak position to stave off a proxy fight—especially when an insurgent group has substantially more shares than management controls.

5. *Low return on equity:* When companies show a low return on the capital employed in the business, an insurgent may be attracted by the possibility of improving the operation and getting a better return on the company's assets, or using them in other ways.

6. *Poor earnings record:* Companies whose profits have been in a decline or whose profits do not compare favorably with those of their competitors are open to charges of improper management. The poorer the company's results, the better the opportunity for outsiders to gain control under the banner of being able to do a better job.

7. *Low dividend payout without good use for retained earnings:* Companies that are growing rapidly can justify low dividends because the money is being put to work in the business. But companies that accumulate cash without good reason are open to charges that they are not giving stockholders a sufficient share of the profits. An insurgent group waging a proxy fight might promise to increase the dividend payout—if elected.

8. *Stock selling at a low price-earnings ratio:* Low price-earnings ratios give insurgents the comfortable feeling that should their plans go awry they can sell the shares they have accumulated with a minimum of loss. Moreover, low price-

earnings stocks are potentially high price-earnings stocks—a siren's song to many outside groups.

9. *Dissatisfied board of directors:* Whenever a board of directors is unhappy with its company's president, there may be a few disgruntled directors—especially outside directors—who can be convinced that an insurgent group seeking to gain control of the company can do a better job than present management.

How To Avoid a Proxy Battle. In addition to the shares the opposition will control on the one side and the stock that management controls on the opposing side will be stock owned by unallied, uncommitted stockholders. To help management win over the undecided group of shareholders, these internal factors should be considered:

MANAGEMENT OWNERSHIP OF STOCK. If company executives and directors do not individually own stock in sizeable amounts, they should begin to buy stock. Aside from the importance of large stock ownership for voting purposes, stock ownership also eliminates the charge that management has no identity of interest with the shareholders and little concern with their welfare.

MANAGEMENT INTEGRITY. Most stockholders are usually inclined to vote with management unless dissidents can prove that management has been working against the stockholders' interest. Consequently, the integrity of management must be beyond question. Management must, for example, avoid transacting business deals with its insiders—company officers, directors, and major stockholders. Moreover, the granting of large bonuses, substantial salary increases, stock options, and other fringe benefits affecting management should be examined beforehand in the light of subsequent charges that may be levelled by the opposition.

PRESTIGE DIRECTORS. When insurgents propose a list of nominees for directors, they will make that list as prestigious as possible, including names that will have appeal to the various segments of stockholder interests. If a company's board can be improved by the addition of names that may impress stockholders, then management should add important directors to the board. Aside from the personal appeal that each director might have, directorships connote a sponsorship of past company activities and are a testimonial to the company's management.

NEW PRESIDENT. If a company is vulnerable to charges of mismanagement or backward management, the company can stifle the charges by electing a new chief executive—even one from the ranks of present management, although it may be more effective to bring in an outsider as president. Every new company head has his own plans, policies, and objectives and can pass off charges against past corporate practices as not being applicable to him. By outlining to stockholders the changed direction that the company will take under his new leadership, the newly appointed chief executive can present alternative plans to current methods as quickly as the opposition will be able to.

NEW PROGRAMS. If it is not feasible to select a new chief executive, the company should re-examine its policies. Possibly the company can change its image—while still keeping its old president—by developing new programs that will be both beneficial to the company and favorably received by the stockholder. Such a course may mean more aggressive marketing policies or the modernization of facilities. If accomplished quickly enough, the company may force insurgents to adopt a "me-too" posture rather than a "you're-wrong" attitude.

CUTS IN LARGE CASH BALANCES OR LARGE CURRENT RATIO. A substantial excess of cash or working capital that is not needed in the business is a prime target for anyone who wishes to gain control of a company. Management ought to determine methods for employing this cash so it is not available for use by an outsider who wants to take over. Some ways to use the excess cash: reinvestment in the company's business, repayment of debt, repurchase of the company's stock, acquisitions for cash, or larger distributions to stockholders, as noted below.

DIVIDEND INCREASE. Every company faced with a proxy fight should re-examine its dividend position. Among the favorite charges in a proxy fight is the claim that management is hoarding its money for its own interests and is not letting stockholders share sufficiently in the profits. If there is a possibility that this charge will come close to the mark, the company should consider an increase in the regular dividend rate. Dividend hikes not only make stockholders feel kindlier towards management because they receive additional income, but also will make it difficult for raiders to promise that they will increase the dividend. If a dividend increase is to be declared, it should be done as far in advance of the start of a proxy fight as possible so stockholders will not get the impression that the dividend is being raised solely as a result of the pressure being placed on management.

STOCK SPLIT. If the price of the stock is selling at a level where a stock split can be justified (see Chapter 2), the company should consider taking such a step. A stock split widens company ownership, making it more difficult and more expensive for insurgents to reach stockholders. A split may also increase the price of the stock—particularly if there has been a thin market and the dividend is simultaneously increased when the stock is split—which will, naturally, make it more costly for the insurgents to buy additional stock.

REDUCTION OF LIQUIDATING VALUE. Stocks that sell below asset value are often prime targets for raiders. Even if raiders honestly do not intend to liquidate the company, liquidation may nonetheless loom as a profitable alternative if the raiders' attempts to improve the company are not successful. If a stock sells at a substantial discount from its asset value, the company may be able to reduce the asset value on the books. Among the ways to do this are: sell off assets that are not needed for the company's operations but that may be on the books at a higher value than their true worth, or write down patents, good will, and other intangible assets if they can be charged directly against surplus.

POTENTIAL ANTI-TRUST SITUATION.   If the insurgent group can be identified—and if it is a corporation that is an important factor in its industry—it may be possible for management to block a takeover attempt by throwing an anti-trust roadblock in the insurgent group's path. Although difficult to accomplish, such a roadblock can be set up by acquiring a company that is directly competitive with the main business of the opposition. If the company that is attempting to gain control is already operating its business under a consent decree, the effectiveness of such an action is all the more certain. However this condition is not necessary for the anti-trust tactic to work. The mere spectre of anti-trust action may be sufficient to disintegrate an insurgent group's power.

DILUTE OPPOSITION'S HOLDINGS.   A company can reduce the voting power of a corporation that has acquired a substantial number of shares by making acquisitions through an exchange of stock. This will result in an increase in the total number of shares outstanding thereby diluting the percentage of stock held by any individual owner or group. Small acquisitions can be made without seeking stockholder approval. Acquisitions that require stockholder ratification will only be successful if the opposition does not have sufficient voting strength to block such a move.

Delaying Strategies.   Since insurgents are typically short of time and money, any action on management's part that will throw the opposition's timetable off schedule or put them to additional expense will work in favor of management. Here are some of the ways a company can capitalize on its opposition's lack of time and money to throw them off balance:

SPECIAL MEETINGS.   Most insurgents try to schedule their take-over program to coincide with the company's annual meeting. Thus, if the company calls a special meeting of stockholders before the regular annual meeting, management can have defensive measures voted on and passed favorably before the opposition is fully organized. The special meeting not only gives the company the chance to change its internal organization but also—since directors will not be elected until the annual meeting—to force the opposition into the expense of two fights instead of one.

LEGAL DELAYING TACTICS. Any insurgent who wants to institute a proxy fight will ask management for a copy of the stockholder list and usually will ask to inspect the company's books and other material that only the company can supply. If the company refuses to comply with such requests, the opposition will naturally have to take the matter to court to force management to comply. Although the courts will rarely uphold the company, forcing each request to court will delay the opposition that much more and force them to spend additional funds.

DEVELOPMENT OF STAGGERED BOARD. For the most part, companies elect all their directors at one time each year. However, in many states it is possible to elect only one-third of the directors annually to serve for three-year terms. Thus for an outside group to gain control of a board, the outsiders would have to win two proxy fights, each battle a year apart. If a company does not have such a staggered board now, management can ask its stockholders to change the bylaws to provide for a staggered board. Calling a special meeting of stockholders (as discussed earlier) is one way to accomplish this before the opposition is effectively organized.

ELIMINATION OF CUMULATIVE VOTING. Managements that are faced with attempts by outsiders to gain representation on the board should attempt to eliminate cumulative voting. Cumulative voting allows a stockholder or a group of stockholders to obtain some representation on a board of directors without having a majority of the stock. Aided by cumulative voting, a stockholder is permitted to multiply his holdings by the number of directors being directed. He then uses his total vote as he wishes. For example: Via cumulative voting, a stockholder group with 100,000 shares in a company that is about to elect nine directors may vote 900,000 shares for one director, vote 100,000 for each of the nine directors, or use the 900,000 votes in any combination.

Girding for a Proxy Contest.   If there is a strong likelihood a proxy contest will soon be launched, the company under attack must prepare to defend itself. Preparation in anticipation of a proxy fight involves not only making provision for the help of outside experts but also for making assignments among top management.

EXECUTIVE ASSIGNMENTS.   The man hours of work involved in a proxy fight are substantial. Executives directly involved in these contests must be prepared to work not only long hours and weekends but also to curtail many of the routine duties surrounding their normal staff activities, such as traveling to various plants or attending regional meetings. Challenges must be answered once a proxy fight has been uncovered, letters have to be drafted, Securities and Exchange Commission clearances must be obtained, and all the while plans must constantly be revised as conditions change.

LEGAL COUNSEL.   Corporate counsel is needed during the proxy contest for instituting actions, for blocking opposition tactics, and for obtaining S.E.C. clearance. If a company's regular counsel is not completely familiar with the rules and the problems involved in proxy contests, his activities should be supplemented with special outside legal counsel which has had proxy-fight experience.

PROXY SOLICITORS.   Obtaining proxies is the most fundamental object in the proxy contest. It is also a specialized assignment. Professional proxy solicitors are needed to pry proxies from thousands of shareholders who never return them and from brokers who do not normally forward them, to obtain proxies favorable to management from as many stockholders as possible, and to check back to make certain that subsequent proxies have not been given to the opposition after the initial one was obtained by the company. It is sometimes worthwhile for management to hire more than one proxy solicitation firm. Since there are only a few professional proxy solicitors, the more management hires, the fewer the opposition can call upon.

ACCOUNTANTS. A company's public auditors as well as its internal accounting department will be called upon during a proxy fight to prepare material to refute certain charges levelled by the opposition. Management should, therefore, see that its accounting staff is adequate to the job soon to be given it. Moreover, management should notify its auditors that the company will expect to have the services of senior accountants available constantly during the proxy battle.

PUBLIC RELATIONS. Whether a company has internal public relations counsel or retains outside counsel, additions to the staff will certainly be necessary during a proxy contest. Aside from increasing the staff size, internal public relations counsel undoubtedly will have to augment its staff with outside financial relations counsel. If the company already retains outside public relations counsel, its staff must not only include those who handle general corporate public relations programs but also those who have familiarity with proxy contests. The problems involved in fighting such battles are considerably different from normal public relations situations and therefore must be handled in different ways.

INVESTIGATION AND ANALYSIS. A substantial amount of research or detective work is usually necessary to probe into the background, past practices, character, and other facets of the group or individual planning to solicit proxies. Such research may often uncover information that can be useful in pointing out to stockholders why they should not give their proxies to the opposition.

Most individuals who try to gain control of a company—although termed "raiders" by management—prefer to consider themselves as knights in shining armor going into battle for the good of all stockholders. It is difficult to avoid a fight with this type of individual. On the other hand, some investors who attempt to take control of a company prefer to do so through a *coup d'état*. They consider proxy fighting beneath their dignity and are much more interested in preserving their respectability.

Although they may threaten a proxy contest to gain representation on a board, they will back away from it when it comes to a showdown with management. Knowledge of the motivation of the individual—or group—trying to gain control can thus help management formulate its strategy.

Getting Stock into Friendly Hands. Obviously, the more votes that management controls, the smaller the possibility that an outsider will challenge management's right to control. If the threat of a proxy fight seems likely, every effort should be made to get as much stock as possible into the hands of investors who can be relied on to be friendly to management.

Getting stock into friendly hands prevents it from falling into the hands of the opposition and reduces the amount of stock available for trading purposes. Such a thinning of the market may cause the price of the stock to rise, making it more expensive for the insurgents to acquire additional shares.

There are several methods by which management can get stock into friendly hands. Among the most popular ways are these:

PURCHASES BY FRIENDS, SUPPLIERS, AND CUSTOMERS. Management should contact personal friends, suppliers to the company, and the company's customers, and ask for their support. The company's suppliers will recognize the importance of continuity of the present management. Some customers may find it important to insure *their* source of supply. And some friends of the company will come to the rescue out of loyalty.

FINANCING EXECUTIVE OPTIONS. Executive stock options that have not yet been exercised are a convenient way for management to acquire additional shares. At times, the possibility of a proxy fight will make the stock sell at a price higher than the option price, making it profitable to exercise the options. Companies can usually arrange with their banks to provide the personal financing an executive may need to exercise his options.

FRINGE BENEFIT PLANS. Many companies' profit-sharing plans and pension plans—with substantial amounts of cash to invest in common stock—allow investments in the company. Such situations are excellent avenues for acquiring stock. Even when the plan is administered by an independent trust department, such as a bank, it can usually be counted on to vote in favor of management. Under employee purchase programs, management generally is the trustee of the stock in that program until the stock has been distributed. As trustee, management is permitted to vote such stock.

PARTIALLY OWNED COMPANY.   A company that is partially owned by another company—but usually less than majority owned—can own the stock of a parent company and is permitted to vote the stock independently. Thus, if the affiliate has enough capital to acquire stock, it can provide an excellent source of management support.

INSTITUTIONS.   While institutional investors typically shun proxy fights, they usually side with management. If a company has convincing plans for its future growth, it may be able to prevail upon some institutional investors to take a position in the company's stock and to side with management. Where an institutional investor already holds some of the company's stock, the company should try—if the institution seems to be friendly to management—to interest it in buying more shares.

ACQUISITION.   Once a company discovers that a proxy fight is in the offing, management may be able to arrange additional stock outstanding—and in friendly hands—by acquiring quickly a smaller company in exchange for stock. If ownership of the acquired company is concentrated among relatively few shareholders, the company should easily be able to determine from discussions with those shareholders whether or not their support can be counted on. To avoid a legal problem, any acquisition ought to be justifiable in terms of the company's normal business operation.

ADDING LARGE STOCKHOLDERS TO THE BOARD.   Naming a large stockholder—or his representative—to the company's board of directors is one way of helping to avoid future problems. This may block the opposition from winning over that stockholder to its side, and may gain his support if a proxy fight erupts sometime in the future.

THE TENDER OFFER

Targets for Tender Offers.   A tender offer is a technique that can be used to take over a well-managed company as well as one with a poor financial record. Companies that are leaders in their respective industries can be the object of a tender offer, particularly if they have something unique that another company believes it can exploit to its advantage. For example, a raw material producer might seek to gain control, by a tender offer, of a company that could be a captive customer for its products. Or a company that needs an established sales organization in a field it plans to enter may seek to take over, via a tender offer, a company with such a sales group.

Offsetting the Tender Offer.   Tender offers are tough to beat. The price offered for the stock is usually sufficiently above the market price to make stockholders waiver in their allegiance to the company. Many techniques used to fight a proxy fight can be adapted to fight a tender offer. In addition, to minimize the threat of a surprise tender offer, and to fight one once it occurs, a company can follow these broad avenues:

RECEPTIVITY TO ACQUISITION OFFERS.   It is wisest for a company to always maintain an open-door policy to legitimate merger or acquisition feelers. While some companies do have a rigid attitude against being acquired, it is nevertheless important that they do not develop a reputation of *never* entertaining an acquisition offer. Such a reputation may force a company wishing to acquire the non-acquisition minded company into making a surprise tender offer. But if a company is willing to listen to legitimate acquisition offers, it may be alerted to a potential tender offer in advance.

PREPARATION OF ALTERNATIVES.   Any management that thinks it might be subject to a tender offer should consider initiating merger talks with companies other than the company seeking control. If a tender offer is subsequently made, the company under attack can conclude a preliminary agreement and offer its stockholders an alternative. On the other hand, if the tender offer does not occur, the merger can be reappraised.

RAISING STOCK PRICE ABOVE TENDER OFFER. Getting friends, suppliers, customers or others to buy stock can defeat a tender offer in one of two ways. First, if the buying raises the market price above the tender price, few people will offer their stock. And, second, if the buying does not raise the market price above the tender offer, the friendly group will accumulate many of the shares that would have gone to the group trying to gain control.

HINDRANCE OF FINANCING. One defensive tactic, if the corporation trying to gain control has to borrow funds to pay for the tendered stock, is to try to convince their banks or other lenders to drop their financial support.

COUNTEROFFER FOR STOCK. A company can schedule a special stockholders' meeting to obtain approval to make an offer for its own shares at a price higher than the tender offer. A willingness to outbid the opposition will discourage most corporations seeking control. The Standard Products Company won shareholder approval to top the offer by American Steel & Pump Corp., which was originally at $13.50 and was subsequently raised to $15. The company defeated the tender proposal by buying nearly 300,000 shares of its own stock at $17.25.

STOCK IN TRANSIT. If feasible, a stock split may be declared, and stockholders can be requested to mail their certificates to the transfer agent to be exchanged for new shares. By having stockholders turn in old certificates for new ones, their stock will be in transit for a considerable period and, therefore, not available for tender. Normally, in a split, stockholders keep their old shares, and the transfer agent issues additional certificates.

BUYING STOCK FROM ARBITRAGEURS. A company that is attacked through a tender offer should remember that it has an opportunity to purchase stock from arbitrageurs, Wall Street professionals who accumulate large blocks of stock in the open market. The arbitrageurs can buy this stock because as the market price rises close to the price of the tender offer, many stockholders will sell their stock rather than wait the additional time to tender their shares for the small extra profit. Arbitrageurs usually will sell the stock they have purchased to the company making the tender offer, often for profits involving only pennies per share, *unless they get a better offer from someone else.*

STOCKHOLDER RELATIONS IN DEFENDING CONTROL

The ultimate test of the effectiveness of a company's financial and stockholder relations program occurs when another corporation tries to gain control of the company. No matter what has gone before, the stockholder program should be reviewed to rectify any deficiencies. In addition to normal stockholder relations procedures, there are certain steps that management should take with its stockholders specifically in connection with a proxy fight or tender offer.

Proxy Fights. FREQUENT MAILINGS. Since stockholders always have the right to revoke their proxy, the last dated proxy is the one that counts. Therefore, it is best to prepare a series of letters to be sent to stockholders to solicit their proxies frequently. Every proxy solicitation sent by the opposition should be immediately matched by still another proxy solicitation from management, since some stockholders sign and return *every* proxy sent to them. Furthermore, the company should time its final proxy solicitation so that its proxy is the last one that stockholders will have an opportunity to mail.

PRIVATE MEETINGS WITH LARGE STOCKHOLDERS. In addition to the calls that the professional proxy solicitor makes on stockholders, top company executives should visit large stockholders personally to explain the company's position and to convince them why their best interests lie with present management. Since the insurgents will probably be calling on those same stockholders, management may have to make more than one visit to overcome whatever arguments the opposition may have stated.

SMALL REGIONAL MEETINGS. Management should hold small, private luncheons with six to ten investors wherever there is a geographic concentration of stockholders with medium-sized holdings. While the size of the holdings of those stockholders might not justify personal visits by management, the combined holdings of several of them may be substantial.

The luncheon invitations should be made personally— preferably by telephone, with a follow-up letter. The telephone approach is best because it will enable the caller to spot any antagonism the stockholder may have toward the company. If the stockholder is disgruntled, he should *not* be invited to the luncheon lest he influence the attitudes of other stock-holders. It is best for management to deal with antagonistic stockholders on an individual personal-visit basis.

MEETINGS WITH BROKERS AND INVESTMENT ADVISORS. This group can have a great deal of influence in a proxy fight. Its recommendations as to how to vote can be the deciding factor. Any broker or advisor who has customers or clients with large holdings should be visited privately.

IDENTIFYING STOCKHOLDERS USING BROKER'S OR NOMINEE'S NAME. It is difficult to reach stockholders who hold stock in the name of a brokerage firm or a nominee. Proxy material will be forwarded to them, but such communications can be de-layed. More important, there may be large stockholders who own stock in "street name" whom company executives will want to visit personally. Uncovering these big stockholders is vital.

To get the names of many of the "street name" stockholders, one company sent a special package of its consumer products to all its stockholders, along with an individual letter from the president. At the same time, the company sent letters to brokers and nominees that held company stock and asked them to forward a letter to the beneficial stockholders they represented. The letter to be forwarded pointed out that other stockholders were receiving a package of the company's product and that even though their holdings were in "street name," management would be happy to send them a package as well. To get the package, the stockholder simply had to list his name and address on an enclosed reply post-card so the company could forward him the free gift. A substantial majority of street-name stockholders replied, enabling the company to obtain their names and addresses.

While that technique does not reveal how many shares each of the stockholders own, follow-up interviews by professional proxy solicitors often can determine the approximate size of their holdings.

Dealing with Tender Offers. Many of the same general stockholder relations principles for a proxy contest also apply in a tender offer situation. These include frequent mailings, retaining proxy solicitors, and individual and group meetings. The basic difference is in the action expected of the stockholder and the arguments used to convince him. In a proxy fight, the stockholder is asked to vote for management rather than for someone else. In a tender offer the stockholder is asked by management not to tender his stock and to thereby forego an immediate financial gain.

Speed is essential in fighting a tender offer. The amount of time available to a company, once a tender offer has been made, is rarely more than a few weeks. Telegrams and phone calls may have to replace letters and meetings. Whatever action a company decides to take in fighting a tender offer, it must gird itself to act quickly.

The company must convince its stockholders that their stock inherently is worth more than the price they will receive by accepting the tender offer. This is a difficult task since the corporation trying to gain control will offer to pay a considerable premium over market price. To overcome this problem, a company must convincingly show why the tender offer is too low a price to accept, and why even greater profits should accrue in the future as a result of holding the stock. There are many ways to do this, and each company will have to find its most effective selling point.

Some of the arguments that can be used are: new products in the laboratory that hold tremendous promise, the possibility of an offer by a third party to purchase the company at a price higher than the tender offer (and perhaps on a tax-free basis), plans for acquisitions that will increase the company's value, forthcoming dividend increases, stock selling well under book value, underlying values that do not appear on the books, or a new market just unfolding.

7

The Corporate Name

It comes as no surprise to management when its company outgrows its manufacturing facilities. With equal ease, a company can outgrow its corporate name. But while managements are quick to spot and rectify the problems caused by production limitations, too often these same executives fail to recognize that an outmoded name may be limiting their companies in other areas—such as their relationship with the investment community.

When a company outgrows its name, the name should be changed. Ideally, the new name that management chooses should describe what the company does. If this is impractical for any reason, then management must make the name have a meaning of its own. Typically, this can be done through an extensive advertising and promotion campaign.

Today there is scarcely a corporation listed on the New York Stock Exchange that has not undergone at least one name change since it was founded. Roughly 150 corporations listed on the New York Stock Exchange assumed new corporate titles within a recent seven-year span.

Even so, there are still a substantial number of major, publicly held companies that are handicapped for lack of an appropriate title. Management's willingness to live with an outmoded name is usually due to the fear that the name's good-will and recognition will be lost. To put the problem in per-spective, this temporary loss of good-will must be pitted against the problems surrounding an outgrown name.

Naturally, the decision to change a name should never be made lightly. Nor should the assignment of finding the correct name ever be considered an easy one. One important reason for a serious approach to finding a new name is that the price at which a company's stock sells can be influenced by a name, which in turn can have an important bearing on the cost of raising new capital or the cost of an acquisition through an exchange of stock.

OUTMODED NAMES

An outmoded name is one that no longer serves a main corporate purpose—such as accurately defining the company's sphere of operations. The problems associated with an incor-rect name are readily seen in the following examples:

1. Oklahoma City–Tulsa Airline at one time served that area spelled out in its corporate title and was thus aptly named. As its operations broadened the company went through four name changes. Today it is called Braniff Airways, Inc.
2. The changing nature of the business of Owens-Illinois, Inc., can be traced through successive name changes before the current name was selected as a result of its diversified opera-tions. The company started out in business as the Owens Bottle Machine Co., changed to the Owens Bottle Co., and then became Owens-Illinois Glass Co.
3. Colt Industries, Inc., changed its name from Fairbanks Whit-ney Corp. when new management wanted to dissociate itself from past problems of the company.

How Names Become Outmoded. Few of the founders of what are today major corporations were able to foresee the growth in size and scope that their fledgling operations would one day achieve. Consequently, the names of their companies often reflected the more modest horizons of the founder, such as a narrow sphere of operations, a specific geographic community, or some other confining designation. Unfortunately, as these companies grew—as they diversified into related but broader activities or shifted their emphasis into new and entirely unrelated fields—their corporate names stood still. Many company names that were appropriate when they were first adopted no longer have their original significance. Some names, as a result of changes in the corporate character, are actually *misleading*.

Dangers in Misleading Names.   An inappropriate name hurts a company's relationship with the financial community.

CLASSIFICATION BY SECURITY ANALYSTS.   The wrong name often puts the company under the jurisdiction of the wrong security analyst. On the surface it may appear that such a confused state is unlikely. Such is far from true. The situation usually develops in the following manner.

When Ajax Metals Company—to use a hypothetical company—made nothing but small metal products, the metals industry analyst followed Ajax, and dozens of other metal manufacturers. A few years ago, Ajax diversified into electronic circuitry and soon the company's income from metal products accounted for a mere fraction of total income. At that point, the metal analyst should have turned over his file on Ajax Metals to the electronic analyst. Typically, he did not. Without a motivating force to cause such a change, a stock usually remains in the category in which it started.

It is easier for Wall Street to accept the company's assessment of itself—as evidenced by its name—than to determine the composition of a company's income. This is particularly true if the company is a small or medium-size one. If one of the three or four largest companies in an industry changed its markets, the investment community would be quicker to catch up with the change despite an outmoded name.

INDUSTRY CLASSIFICATION AND PRICE-EARNINGS RATIO.   The industry in which a company is classified is one of the most important influences on the price-earnings ratio at which a stock sells. Each industry has its own price-earnings range. For example, stocks of companies in the electronics industry usually can be expected to sell at a price-earnings ratio more than twice that of the metals industry. The disadvantage of an electronics company that is classified as a metals company is obvious.

Comparative financial ratios published both in the press and in surveys published by investment firms may indicate the company is out of line with its industry. Yet, those published ratios may not be pertinent if the company has been grouped with the wrong industry.

CLASSIFICATION BY THE PRESS. A wrong name can cause problems with the financial press. As the reporting coverage of the business and financial scene has expanded—by specialized investment publications, financial sections of leading metropolitan newspapers and trade journals—reporters and editors have been assigned to cover specific industries. If a company's name links it to a particular business, the company may be included in industry stories where it does not belong. More importantly, a company may be omitted from stories in which it should be included.

PROBLEMS IN SELECTING A NAME

There are some traps a company can fall into in selecting a new name. The following should be considered in any such name-selecting decision:

Initials and Abbreviations. Management ought to be wary of adopting a set of initials in lieu of a full name. Initials tend to be confusing and are difficult to remember. While International Business Machines or Radio Corporation of America could use initials for their names without meeting any problems, most companies are not in a similar situation. PHP Co., AMK Corp., GTI Corp., NRM Corp., and FWD Corp. are just a sprinkling of the more than 400 initial-named, publicly held companies that literally challenge investors to decipher what they do.

On the other hand, a long name invariably is abbreviated by others, and a company should try to anticipate what the abbreviation might be. Such foresight could eliminate a name whose abbreviation would conflict with another's trademark or trade name. Just think of the problems a company would encounter if it changed its name to Central Business Service.

Fashions in Industry Identification. A company should avoid picking a name solely to ride the coat tails of an industry currently popular with investors. If it does, it will eventually regret trying to capitalize on investor fervor by stretching its corporate identity to include the name of an industry that is not realistically its business. When such an industry falls out of investor favor the company will suffer as much as if it belonged to the industry.

NAME CHANGE FOLLOW-UP

Changing a company's name to have it reflect operations more realistically is only the start of obtaining proper investor recognition. An active program must be instituted to make sure that the objectives which initiated a name change in the first place are accomplished.

A new name is a good starting point for overcoming the tradition and inertia that may have kept a company assigned to the wrong security analysts or financial reporters. The company must then take the initiative in working with these groups to see that the responsibility is reassigned to the proper person and the company analyzed and reported on in the proper context.

8

Investment Banking Relations

One of the most important financial decisions that a company will make—a decision affecting both its raising of capital and its relationship with the investment community—is the selection of an investment banker. The decision is an important one because the financial community uses the reputation of the company's investment banker to size up a company intuitively. Wall Street invariably knows which investment bankers demand the highest financial and ethical standards and which use less exacting criteria when accepting companies to underwrite. Thus, a company can unwittingly tarnish its standing on Wall Street by settling for an investment banker of low caliber. A company must be selective and—within the framework of its own financial stature—get the best investment banker possible.

A well-regarded investment banking institution is equally as concerned that any company whose stock it underwrites be a sound company. When an investment banking firm underwrites an issue, that firm is quite literally putting its seal of approval on the company and its stock. In effect, the investment banker tells the investment community that the company whose stock is being underwritten has been thoroughly investigated and has passed muster. If the company is not a sound, well-run company, the investment banking firm's reputation will suffer. A few poor underwritings are all that is needed for Wall Street to lower its opinion of an investment banker.

Consequently, all investment bankers have standards that a company must meet before they will underwrite an issue. Such standards vary widely; the better bankers, naturally, have the more stringent standards. The successful mating of company and investment banker is a long, complex procedure. This Chapter examines that relationship from both partners' points of view.

ROLE OF INVESTMENT BANKER

An investment banker assists in filling the capital requirements of business by obtaining funds, usually on a permanent or long-term basis. It is, in effect, the middleman between corporate issuers of securities and the ultimate investors— individual and institutional. Established organizations; new or expanding companies; reorganized, merged, or consolidated firms; and governmental units look to the investment banker for the financing of their capital requirements. The investment banker's primary source of income is the margin of profit, or spread, between the price at which it buys securities from businesses and the price at which it resells them to the investing public. Investment bankers typically will accept a narrower profit margin when underwriting a well-known, highly regarded company and demand wider profit margins when selling the stock of a fledgling company.

Since the investment banking field is highly competitive, investment bankers offer—in varying degrees—many services to their clients in addition to the raising of long-term capital. As with all business concerns, some investment bankers do a better job than others in performing the many services they promise. And—to a noticeable extent—they in general tend to concentrate on those services that may lead to additional profits for themselves. For example, assisting in mergers and acquisitions is one typical service that generates extra money—via a finder's fee—for the investment banker.

Raising Capital. There are several ways in which an investment banker provides the financing for a company's capital requirements:

STOCKS, BONDS, AND COMMERCIAL PAPER. Underwriting a common stock issue is undoubtedly the most usual way in which an investment banker raises money for its client. The underwriter and the company agree on the price at which the company will sell the stock to the underwriter and the underwriter will resell to the public. Assisting in the selling of the stock may be other investment bankers that share the underwriting risk and help to widen geographic distribution of the stock.

Investment bankers also raise capital on a long-term debt basis via corporate bonds. The investment banker will counsel the company on the length of the bond, its coupon rate, etc. —all with an eye toward raising money at the lowest possible cost.

Some investment bankers—although not many—sell commercial paper for their clients to raise short-term money. The terms of such notes usually range from 30 to 90 days. Large companies with heavy seasonal requirements for funds frequently find commercial paper sales an excellent source of temporary capital.

When corporate securities are offered to stockholders on a rights basis, an investment banker will guarantee to take over any securities not purchased by the stockholders. Operating on such a stand-by basis, investment bankers provide insurance to the company that the issue will be completely sold.

CONTACTS WITH INSTITUTIONAL INVESTORS AND COMMERCIAL BANKS. Investment bankers know the requirements of institutional investors and the best methods of obtaining funds from this source. Consequently, investment bankers are able to arrange for direct placement of equity securities or—more commonly—for long-term borrowing on a straight-debt basis, a mortgage, a sale-leaseback, or some other form of financing.

As companies grow, their commercial banking needs change. An investment banker can be helpful in guiding companies to those banks best suited to them.

Other Services. In addition to raising capital, many investment bankers also provide other kinds of assistance. While a secondary sale of a company's common stock (generally by major stockholders) puts no money in the company's bank account, a good or poor underwriting of the secondary sale can help or hurt the company's stock. The underwriting of a secondary issue by an investment banker requires as much skill and financial knowhow as that of an issue to raise new capital.

Since investment bankers have financial contacts in many diverse business areas they often are able to bring companies seeking acquisitions together with those willing to be acquired. Many investment bankers have special departments to provide this kind of service. In addition to finding companies for acquisitions or mergers, they often assist in actual negotiations of the price and terms.

Investment bankers frequently try to interest institutions in taking a position in the stock of one of their clients. When an institution decides to purchase a large block, the investment banker will work closely with it to obtain the stock for its portfolio. Conversely, if an institution that already owns stock decides to sell, the investment banker will try to arrange the sale so that it will have the least negative effect on the price of the stock.

Over-the-counter dealers across the country can frequently be persuaded by investment bankers to make a market in a client's stock, assuming, of course, the stock is not listed. In addition, the investment banker itself will usually make a market in the stock.

An investment banker can advise a company on a multitude of subjects apart from—but certainly related to—the financial aspects of the corporation. Frequently, an investment banking partner will sit on the board of a client company. Such an arrangement allows the company to obtain the partner's counsel on a regular and continuing basis.

A firm that wishes to list on a securities exchange will find its investment banker able to assist it in receiving informal preliminary approval. Once informal approval has been granted, the investment banker will help the company prepare its listing applications and see that all requirements are met.

YARDSTICKS FOR SELECTING INVESTMENT BANKERS

There are many levels in the hierarchy of investment banking firms. Although the particular notch in which a firm belongs is not written down anywhere—and there might be some minor disagreement among individuals as to the specific classification of a firm—there is a remarkable consensus among knowledgeable Wall Streeters.

Despite the ease with which the top investment banking firms can be identified, not every company can choose the firm with which it wishes to do business. Such is the case simply because—as noted earlier—the investment banker also retains the right to accept or reject a client on the basis of its own standards. It naturally behooves a company to select the best possible investment banking firm within its own financial league. All too frequently, a good company settles for a lesser grade investment banker because it has not been sufficiently aggressive in finding one to match its own caliber. Some yardsticks for use in finding the right investment banker follow.

Reputation. Since each investment banker has a distinct and almost universally accepted reputation in the financial community, it is a relatively easy matter to locate the standing of any specific investment banking firm. Obvious sources for such advice are a company's commercial bank, officers of major corporations who have been dealing with investment bankers over the years, and other disinterested individuals who have a good knowledge of Wall Street. One not so obvious source—but in many instances the best one—of a candid appraisal of an investment banker is one of the better investment banking firms. While the investment banker may glorify his own firm's position, he will generally classify other firms properly.

National or Regional Firms.   The leading underwriters are national, and almost all have their headquarters in New York City. Yet, there are many excellent regional investment banking houses that are located outside of New York. A company planning to sell a comparatively small issue might do better to use the services of a good regional investment banker—especially if the company's reputation or business is chiefly local. While that company's long-range objective might be to secure a broad geographic diversification of stockholders, it might achieve that goal faster through the intermediate step of a good regional underwriting firm.

Underwriting Experience with Similar Issues.   Some investment bankers have tended to specialize in particular industries or in companies with similar growth patterns. If a company can locate an investment banker whose specialization matches its own characteristics, that firm—all other things being equal —will make a good candidate for consideration.

Investment Banker's Size Requirements.   Many investment bankers set standards as to the smallest company they will underwrite. Some of the larger underwriters insist that a company have $1 million in earnings, after taxes, before they will consider becoming its investment banker.

When looking for an investment banker, a company must think in terms of the dollar amount of its issue. The larger the issue, the better the chance of securing a good firm to underwrite the offering. Since many firms have minimum requirements, a small issue will automatically eliminate certain of them. On the other hand, a large issue may eliminate smaller underwriters since they will have inadequate capital to handle a large offering properly. The size of other issues that an investment banker has underwritten is probably the best guide to estimating its requirements.

Amount and Kind of Compensation. Typically, the larger the dollar amount to be underwritten, the lower will be the overall commission as a percentage of the total underwriting. Moreover, the better the investment banker, the lower will be the underwriting commission. The better firms generally charge an underwriting commission in the vicinity of 10% or lower.

Large companies with sound finances should be able to raise capital less expensively than the smaller companies. Such is the case because smaller companies require greater efforts to sell the securities and the degree of risk assumed by the investment banker is much greater. One word of caution: When the underwriting commission approaches 15% of the total underwriting, the company should seriously re-examine its decision to sell stock.

In addition to underwriting commissions, some investment bankers ask for other compensation. Among the extras they may seek are (1) the purchase of stock by the underwriter at a price *below* the public offering price, (2) the granting of options or warrants on the stock to the investment banker, and (3) management or consulting fees. A value must be placed on these extras to get the true underwriting cost.

Pricing and Timing Policies. An underwriter usually determines the price at which it wants to sell a new issue with two things in mind: The price should be low enough to make it easily marketable and represent an attractive purchase to potential buyers, and the price should be high enough to compensate the company or the selling stockholders adequately. Generally, an underwriter is in a better position than company executives or selling stockholders to establish a fair price. However, if there is wide disagreement on the value of the securities to be sold, then the underwriter obviously is not the right one for the company.

An investment banker may insist on waiting for better stock market conditions before underwriting a company's issue. Even under favorable circumstances, he might counsel the company to wait until it has achieved higher earnings before an offering is made to the public. Underwriting is a risky business, and some investment bankers are willing to take greater risks than others. If the company is not satisfied with the timing an investment banker insists upon in bringing an issue to market and is convinced of the validity of its position, it should seek an investment banker with whom it is more in agreement.

Post-offering Follow-Through.   All investment bankers promise to work actively for the company's interest after the offering is completed. Unfortunately, many of these promises are not adequately fulfilled. Even some of the widely respected investment bankers fall down on the job for certain of their clients. This sometimes occurs in the case of the smaller companies they represent who get neglected because of the amount of attention paid to larger, more important clients. If a company will end up as one of an investment banker's smaller clients, the company should do some research on the amount of continuing support it can expect. One good way is to talk to other companies of similar size that are clients of that underwriter to learn of their experience.

CHANGING INVESTMENT BANKERS

When a company outgrows its investment banker, it is time to change to another more suitable firm. It is not unusual for a company to outgrow an investment banker. As companies expand their operations and become more profitable, their stature in the financial community becomes greater and their requirements become greater. If the company has grown while the investment banking firm has remained relatively stable, the capabilities of the investment banker will no longer be adequate to fill the company's needs. This situation is especially true when the investment banking firm is a regional one and the company has developed national recognition.

Obstacles to Change.   While it is not difficult for a company to outgrow the investment banker, it is not common to switch from one to another. Although an investment banking connection does not have to be a permanent one, in practice it often works out that way. Factors such as these frequently obscure the need for a change:

1. *Loyalty:* The financial community expects a company to maintain a degree of loyalty to its investment banker simply because—if for no other reason—that banker did perform an important service for the company when that help was needed.

2. *Valuable counsel:* Since the relationship between the investment banker and the company is often a close one, the company may have become quite dependent on the expertise of the investment banker. As a result, the company may be reluctant to switch investment bankers.

3. *Investment banker on the board:* Whenever a partner of the investment banking house is a member of the company's board of directors, it is awkward to change investment bankers.

4. *Contract provisions:* Some investment bankers have contracts with their client-companies stating that the company must offer the banker any future underwriting for a period of several years on a first-refusal basis.

When To Change.   Despite all these considerations, a company should change investment bankers when the need actually exists—although where there is a contractual arrangement, the company will have to live up to, as best it can, the terms of that contract. There are times, however, when a true need does not exist. Management must be cognizant of the fact that, as with any close relationship, minor frictions between the company and the investment banker can and will develop. This alone should not be cause for shifting investment bankers.

The advice that a company gets from its investment banker may not always coincide with the thinking of company executives. This is not at all surprising. Company executives tend to be internally oriented while investment bankers tend to think more in terms of the investing public. Although their ultimate responsibilities and objectives are the same, their divergent backgrounds may produce different ways of approaching the same problem.

On the other hand, if a company believes that the investment banker is not performing the follow-through functions originally promised—or is doing so in a lackadaisical manner —it should bring it to the investment banker's attention. An investment banker should not be permitted to become complacent and shirk the work expected of it. Investment bankers are in a highly competitive industry and will react to pressure on them to perform as they promised. A company should bear in mind, though, that the more financial rewards it can offer the investment banker the more activity it can expect to receive. (See below, page 99, for a discussion of how to use company-generated brokerage commissions to reward investment bankers.)

Management should be aware that it cannot change investment bankers with any degree of frequency. Wall Street considers frequent changes from one investment banker to another an undesirable characteristic, and fickle companies will soon find better investment banking firms shying away from them. Frequent changes create more problems than they solve.

Handling a Change.   When a company's relationship with its investment banker has been a good one, but a new investment banker is nevertheless required, the change can be made smoothly. In fact, a good investment banker will understand the company's need for a bigger investment banker and many times will cooperate with the company in making a change. To further ensure that the situation is properly handled, the following should be undertaken by the company:

1. *Discuss problem with current investment banker:* The subject of selecting a new investment banker should be discussed thoroughly with the original underwriter. If the need truly exists, that underwriter may be the first to recognize the necessity of a change and may even waive whatever contractual arrangement exists between the two parties.

2. *Ask investment banker to help find new underwriter:*
The company's investment banker should be asked to recommend firms that might possibly suit the company's new requirements. At the same time, certainly, the company should seek the advice of others in the financial community. After having interviewed prospective investment bankers, the company should again consult its current one for its advice before making a final decision.

3. *Keep original investment banker on the board:* If a partner of the original investment banker is on the company's board and his advice has been valuable, he should be asked to remain as a director, even if a representative of the company's new investment banker is to be elected to the board.

4. *Arrange for original investment banker to participate in financing:* As a good-will gesture, a company usually can arrange with its new investment banker for the original investment banker to be a major participant in future underwritings and—if at all possible—to be a joint manager of future offerings. Management should explain to the original underwriter that the company intends to request this procedure, which should do much to smooth acceptance of the change. Management should also discuss with potential new underwriters their attitudes toward such an arrangement.

DIRECTING COMMISSIONS TO INVESTMENT FIRMS

The brokerage commissions generated by transactions in securities that a company controls can be used to compensate an investment banker—as well as others in the financial community—for their services. These commissions, which can amount to substantial sums of money, can help pay for corporate obligations at no cost to the company.

Specifically, many companies have pension or profit sharing funds managed by bank trust departments or investment advisors. Too often, management fails to designate the brokerage firms through which the shares should be bought and sold. As a result, a company loses a free opportunity of rewarding

—via stock commissions—Wall Street firms that have been helpful to the company.

The Investment Banker.   The fairest way to judge how much commission business the company's investment banker should receive is to evaluate the benefits the company is getting from the investment banker in relation to the compensation the investment banker is receiving from the company. For example, if a recent underwriting resulted in a large fee, the commissions directed to the investment banker may be proportionately less. Similarly, fees in connection with acquisitions or mergers or financial consulting retainers should be taken into account when deciding how much commission business ought to be given to the investment banker.

However, it is just as likely that the company is already receiving *greater* benefits from the relationship than is the investment banker. The value of the latter's time and effort expended should, therefore, be carefully weighed in calculating the commissions to be directed.

Other Investment Firms.   Although a company's investment banker may be the sole recipient of a company's commission business, other brokerage firms sometimes deserve to be included.

Among other brokerage firms that might receive directed commission business from a company are those:

1. That have demonstrated a long and continuing interest in the company
2. Active in bringing potential acquisitions to the attention of the company
3. That keep the company alerted to industry and competitive developments and trends
4. That took an interest in the company when it was small and others were ignoring it
5. That maintained their loyalty and faith in the company when it was going through a difficult period
6. Situated in the company's local area and that have demonstrated a semi-parental interest in the progress of the company
7. Situated in geographically wide-spread areas and that have

been instrumental in helping the company obtain national recognition

8. That have performed some other service to the company for which they deserve additional compensation

The designation of brokerage firms to receive commissions should be solely in light of long-term relationships that have developed. *Under no circumstances should commissions be given to a brokerage firm for recommending the company's stock or for purchasing stock for its own account.* Extreme care must be exercised on the part of management to insure that the allocation of commission business could not possibly be construed as a reward for such practices.

Discretion in Placing Commission Business.   Banks and investment advisers should be given some discretion in placing orders with non-designated brokers. However, these deviations should be permitted only when results can be obtained that cannot be through company-designated brokers. A limited degree of commission discretion given to a bank will work to the company's advantage. For example, if a brokerage firm not on the company's list has a large block of a stock for sale, the bank may be able to buy the issue through that firm at a lower price than through a company-designated firm. A similar benefit might be achieved when the bank—in purchasing an over-the-counter stock—can obtain a better price from a dealer making a primary market in the stock.

Investment advisers and bank trust departments naturally prefer a free hand in placing commission business. It enables them to gain advantages that the company should be receiving. For example, banks use stock commissions as a reward to their brokerage clients who maintain compensating balances with the bank. Nevertheless, almost all banks will comply with company instructions to direct commissions.

An annual evaluation should be made to see that the company's instructions have been carried out. The amount of commission business that the company allocates to each brokerage firm should also be reviewed each year.

9

Financial Relations Counsel

Management has recognized financial relations as a distinct and separate corporate activity for only little more than a decade. The rapid growth of this new and highly specialized profession has stemmed from management's increasing awareness of the need to communicate with stockholders, the professional investment community, the financial press, and the governmental and semi-public agencies that regulate issuing of and trading in securities.

The individual responsible for setting financial relations policy is the company's chief executive. But he cannot do this job alone since usually he has neither the time nor the specialized background required. He must employ—in varying degrees, depending on his attitudes, interest, and training—the professional capabilities and knowledge of the executives on his staff, including the financial vice president, treasurer, and secretary, as well as the company's auditors, investment banker, internal or external legal counsel, internal or external public relations counsel, and internal or external financial relations counsel.

This Chapter is concerned with the role and function of the internal or external financial relations counsel. The individuals on the staffs of either are—or should be—professional specialists who understand the investment community and how best to bridge the gap between the company and Wall Street.

ADVANTAGES OF OUTSIDE COUNSEL

While many companies have attempted to solve the problem of communicating with Wall Street by employing financial relations specialists as part of the company's staff, the use of outside financial relations consultants is accepted practice today for many corporations. The trend, unquestionably, has been for greater use of outside financial relations consultants for the following reasons:

Program Conducted at Top Level. The chief executive of a corporation rarely gives the type of authority necessary to conduct a financial relations program to someone relatively low in the company's hierarchy. Typically, the internal financial relations staff is brought up to date *after* a decision has been reached. Staff members are not normally brought in to advise management on such matters as dividend or acquisition policy before a decision is made. Most top company officers feel more comfortable turning to their outside financial relations consultants to discuss these matters. The consultant has a stature in the eyes of management that an employee almost never achieves—even if he is equally as competent as the outside consultant. The consultant deals with the company's chief executive and the chief financial officer directly, while members of the financial relations staff usually get their information after it has trickled down through several layers of management.

As a result of the outside consultant working at higher executive levels than internal staff members, the consultant has a greater awareness and understanding of the company's financial plans and programs and policies. However, the internal staff usually is more familiar with the day-to-day corporate activities.

Varied Experience and Broad Contacts. Since outside counsel handles the financial relations programs for many corporations, it gains continuing experience over a broad range of subjects. That knowledge and ability can be put to use for the benefit of all its clients. Such wide experience is constantly being added to by the multitude of varied financial problems confronting management. It would not be available to a company if its entire program were handled internally.

Because the work of outside financial relations counsel brings them into contact with many diverse areas of the financial community, the outside counsel is in a better position to know the varied requirements of brokerage houses, institutional investors, security analysts, and financial writers. Thus, the work being done for one client can lay the foundation for an investment firm or financial editor to take an interest in another of the counsel's clients.

Objective Viewpoint. Outside financial relations counsel is not encumbered by being too close to the daily corporate routine. He is able to stand back and observe the company objectively and to see more clearly how the investment community views the company.

Moreover, since the consultant is not a company employee but someone whose livelihood comes from many clients, he can take a strong stand without the fear of losing his job. The staff man, naturally, must be aware that a strong stand may jeopardize his advancement or his employment.

Cost. Most companies with sales under $300 million will find that a financial relations program can be conducted more economically by using outside counsel. Companies with sales exceeding $500 million will usually be able to conduct their own programs at a cost the same as—and sometimes lower than—with outside counsel. For the company with sales between $300 million and $500 million, the economics of using outside counsel will vary. Fees charged by outside consulting firms may range from $1,000 to $3,000 a month or higher. In addition, out-of-pocket expenses may amount to another 20% to 30% of the fee. These figures refer to a financial- and stockholder-relations program and do not include general corporate or other types of public relations.

ROLE OF FINANCIAL RELATIONS CONSULTANT

The financial relations consultant—whether an outside consultant or on the company's staff—advises the company on all aspects of its relationship with the investment community: professional and stockholder investor relations, financial press relations, and financial counseling. Many times the outside consultant provides the staff for the conduct of most of the program. The following explores briefly the several components of a well-run financial relations program:

Professional Investor Relations. In handling a company's contacts with security analysts, financial relations counsel will:

1. *Prepare material for distribution to security analysts:* Such material consists of operating results and other news announcements plus background material about the company.

2. *Serve as a convenient, readily accessible financial information center:* The consultant should have sufficient knowledge of the company's affairs to give immediate and accurate answers to most questions posed by security analysts. When he cannot answer the question, he will get a prompt reply from a company executive and relay the answer to the analyst.

3. *Acquaint analysts with the company:* Security analysts on the staff meet regularly with analysts in the investment community to bring the company to the attention of institutions and brokerage houses that may not have been fully aware of the company's operations and its financial record.

4. *Arrange meetings for corporate executives:* Because it is necessary for company executives to meet in person with security analysts periodically, the financial relations counsel

invites those analysts who will do the most good for the company and arranges for company executives to appear before security analyst groups.

5. *Maintain up-to-date mailing lists:* The consultant maintains mailing lists of those analysts who are—or should be—interested in the company, making prompt corrections as analysts change firms or assignments, and adding new analysts' names to the list as they are brought into the scope of the company's information program.

6. *Know the financial community intimately:* The consultant must be able to direct the program to those specific firms and analysts who should be most interested in knowing about the company. Such intimate knowledge also helps the consultant establish priorities for the amount of time corporate executives devote to various aspects of the program.

Stockholder Relations. The financial relations counsel assists a company in all areas of its relationship with its stockholders. It advises the company on all material to be distributed to stockholders, such as the annual report, interim statements, and other company communications including direct correspondence. Counsel also advises management on how to conduct the annual, regional, and special stockholder meetings.

Financial Press Relations. In dealing with the financial press, counsel prepares and distributes news stories to the proper media, develops feature and interpretive articles on the company, provides background material on the company and industry for the press, and acts as the company's information center for financial editors.

Financial Counseling. The most important function of the financial relations counsel is its advising the company on all internal financial actions that ultimately will affect the company's relationship with the financial community—actions such as reporting of results, dividend increases, stock splits, new financing, and acquisitions.

Getting the Most from Outside Counsel. The best financial relations counsel can be only as effective as the company's cooperation allows. To get the best use of financial relations counsel, management should:

1. Consult with counsel before taking any action that concerns the investment community (To use their services solely to dispense information deprives the company of their full value.)
2. Consider the advice of financial relations counsel in the light of overall corporate policy, not relying on their advice to relieve management from the responsibility of making a decision
3. Keep counsel thoroughly up to date on all corporate developments that will help them interpret the company to the public
4. Keep counsel informed about requests the company gets for information from members of the investment community (Counsel can then supply additional information to those who have shown an interest in the company.)
5. Have financial relations counsel present at meetings between company executives and security analysts (Such a procedure not only enables counsel to know what was talked about but also gives them an opportunity to provide the analyst with additional information after the meeting.)

Standards for Outside Counsel. Management retaining outside financial relations counsel has every right to expect high standards of professional ethical behavior. Among these standards are:

1. Fairness and objectivity in making recommendations to the company and also in distributing information to the financial community
2. Discretion in handling confidential information
3. A thorough and current understanding of company operations
4. A sound knowledge of Securities and Exchange Commission rules and regulations and other laws, rules, and regulations affecting investor relations
5. Prompt action in correcting false or misleading information or rumors about the company
6. Dissemination of corporate information—both favorable and unfavorable—without making recommendations about the company's stock, thereby letting the investment community

make its own appraisal of a company's value in the market place

7. Never exploiting information gained as an "insider" for personal gain

In regard to the last point, while there is no law requiring the principals or staff of a financial relations firm to disclose any of their transactions in a client's stock, some financial relations firms maintain a policy of not permitting any such transactions. These firms do not allow any member of their firm to own, directly or indirectly, the stock of any client they represent.

In the past, some companies paid for all or a part of their financial relations program by granting stock options to the consultant. Such compensation implies that the function of the financial relations program is to raise the price of the company's stock rather than to provide an objective educational and informational program for the investment public. The Public Relations Society of America has this to say:

[A] member shall not accept compensation which would place him in a position of conflict with his duty to his client, employer or the investing public. Specifically, such member shall not accept a contingent fee or a stock option from his client or employer unless part of an over-all plan in favor of corporate executives, nor shall he accept securities as compensation at a value substantially below market price.[1]

A number of leading financial relations firms have imposed upon themselves far stricter codes and are unequivocally opposed to their firms or members of their firms accepting any client company options or securities or contingent fees; they feel this is a questionable practice under any circumstance.

THE CONSULTANT'S STAFF

To conduct a financial relations program effectively, the consultant's staff must have within its ranks specialists in the various areas of financial relations. Without such a knowledgeable and well-rounded staff, the consultant will be able to offer little ad-

[1] Public Relations Society of America, Inc., *Public Relations Register 1967/1968*, Nineteenth Annual Edition, New York, p. 26.

vantage to the company and may inadvertantly create problems due to lack of technical understanding.

Financial Analysts. Executives and staff assigned to handle a financial relations program must have educational background and business experience similar to that of those who work in finance and investments. Individuals trained as security analysts, investment bankers, or investment advisors are probably best prepared to conduct the part of the program dealing with the professional investment community. Since they will be working with security analysts of brokerage firms, investment advisory services, or institutional advisors, they must be trained to talk to them on their own level. Staff members without this background should not be permitted to discuss a company's affairs with security analysts or any other members of the professional investment community. Without specific technical knowledge, misinterpretation of information can easily occur.

Financial Writers. These are financial communications specialists whose background has been financial writing. Financial writers translate management's messages into stories and articles for the nation's financial press. They also prepare stockholder communications and executive speeches, and handle other financial writing assignments.

Financial Counsel. The financial relations staff must include executives who are qualified to advise the company on how its financial decisions—an upcoming merger or methods of raising capital, for example—will affect the attitudes of the investment community towards the company. Needed are men who can tell the company how such actions will affect their investor relationships.

COMBINING OUTSIDE AND INTERNAL STAFFS

Companies large enough to carry out their own financial relations program as economically with an internal staff as with outside counsel have frequently combined the best features by using both.

The internal staff carries out the day-to-day aspects of the financial relations program—particularly in the areas of stockholder communications and the financial press. The outside counsel, on the other hand, works primarily with security analysts and other members of the professional investment community. They are also responsible for the overall development and continuity of the program, for evaluating the program's results, and for advising on all matters handled by the internal staff.

II

SECURITY ANALYSTS AND INSTITUTIONAL INVESTORS

10

Talking to Security Analysts

Every publicly owned company—regardless of size—should establish a policy to specifically name the executives that have the authority to talk with security analysts. Implicit in the policy must be the admonition that all others within that company —such as vice presidents in charge of sales or production, research directors, advertising managers, publicity men—must immediately refer any call from a security analyst to one of the specified company spokesmen.

IMPORTANCE OF POLICY ON COMPANY SPOKESMEN

For anyone who thinks that such a policy is extreme and over-cautious, the following case histories reveal what can happen when individuals other than official spokesmen talk with security analysts.

The secretary to the president of a major Midwestern department store took a long-distance call from a security analyst in New York. She politely informed him that the president was out of town but would be back on the following day. "That's al-right," the analyst said. "I'm checking on the date of your next dividend meeting. It is next Friday, isn't it?" The secretary told him that he was correct.

The analyst asked one more innocent question: "I am pre-paring a bulletin recommending your company that will be is-sued before next Friday. I assume it is safe to say that there will be no change in the dividend?"

That same morning the secretary had typed a memo recom-mending an increase of 10 cents per share in the quarterly divi-dend. Not wanting to reveal confidential information but trying to be helpful, she cautioned the analyst, "You ought to delay your report until after the directors' meeting or leave out any reference to the dividend."

A few of the directors subsequently expressed grave concern that a brokerage house report had stated that the dividend would be increased at the next directors' meeting before the in-crease had even been proposed to them.

In another instance, an investment banker in New York re-ceived a call from a friend in another Wall Street firm asking for information about a paper company of which he is a director. Among the points the director made in trying to be of assistance was that there was every reason to expect continued dividend increases in line with rising profits and the company's policy of paying out 50 per cent of earnings. When the friend's firm pub-lished a report recommending the paper company's stock, one of the things emphasized was an impending liberalization of the dividend.

What neither the director nor the analyst knew was that the executives of the paper company were planning to ask the direc-tors to approve an extensive capital expenditure program that would prohibit any increase in the dividend for the next two years. Many of those who became stockholders because of the expected dividend increase grew discontented when it did not materialize.

Finally, there is the case of a toy manufacturer with plants in six different cities throughout the Southeast. When a plant accounting for 30 per cent of the company's production was hit by fire, a major New York brokerage house attempted to reach a top company officer for a statement. Failing this, they wired a local office near the plant, asking for an investigation of the extent of the damage. The plant manager told the local representative, "The place is in ruins. We'll be out of production for the next six months and will probably miss the whole Christmas selling season." Only hours later the brokerage house wired a new, sharply cut earnings estimate for the company to all branch offices and recommended that customers be advised to sell their stock.

While the brokerage house was writing off the plant, the company president was arranging for double shifts at two other plants and for sub-contracting some of the production. These moves were costly but not nearly as costly as the precipitous drop in the price of the stock—brought on by the plant manager's statement—would seem to have indicated.

Fundamental to each of these case histories is a security analyst who set out to get information that nobody else had. Not all analysts will go to that trouble. In fact, most will not. But the rewards can be great for those who do attempt to be enterprising.

Since such information is worth money to investors, the analysts who regularly come up with fresh information are highly regarded in their profession.

The best way a company can thwart an enterprising analyst who is determined to learn something that is not to be revealed outside the corporate family is to establish a policy that names those who may—and those who may not—talk for the company.

SELECTING COMPANY SPOKESMEN

The Chief Executive. In an ideal situation there is but a single spokesman, the chief executive. This eliminates problems raised by the diverse answers to analysts' questions that are almost inevitable when two or more executives are involved.

Although other officers may be capable of discussing the

company and may be able to respond to specific questions in greater detail, it is the chief executive that most analysts prefer to meet. One reason is that he is in the best position to impart the philosophy of his company. He is often the only officer able to discuss adequately the future direction of the company, general problem areas, and other broad topics that give the analyst an insight into the motives, thinking, and planning behind the company's progress.

Other Executives.   The realities of corporate life usually make the ideal of president as sole spokesman impractical. He may be often away from the office or too busy for interviews. Moreover, he will usually have to check with other company officers in order to answer some of the analysts' more technical questions. It is apparent that the president usually needs help. Who, then, are the best candidates among the other executives for the job of company spokesman?

CHIEF FINANCIAL OFFICER.   The chief financial officer is an obvious and excellent choice, and most companies use him in this capacity at least to some extent. He may talk with analysts only when the president is not available, or they may share the task routinely. In some companies all interviews are directed to the chief financial officer, and the president sees analysts only rarely.

EXECUTIVE VICE PRESIDENT.   The executive vice president makes a good spokesman in the right circumstances. If he is financially oriented he will usually have a sufficiently broad view of the corporation to communicate on the proper level. If he has roots in a field other than finance, some caution should be exercised in naming him as a spokesman. For example, the executive vice president who has risen from the sales area and is still chiefly responsible for sales may have retained a rather narrow perspective on company activities that leaves him not particularly fitted for the role.

EXECUTIVES WITH SPECIAL KNOWLEDGE.   A director of research, a marketing vice president, or some other executive with a specialized function may be the one that an analyst wishes to interview to pursue some particular line of inquiry. While it is perfectly proper to grant this request, the meeting should take place only in the presence of an official spokesman who can exercise some control over the subjects discussed.

Importance of Consistent Statements. It should be reemphasized that when two or more executives are designated to talk with security analysts they must all agree on what is to be revealed and what is not and on how specific items of information are to be handled. Financial officers, for example, who tend in general to be more conservative in their outlook and to hedge their answers more than most other executives, should be sure that the estimates of future prospects they give agree with those of other spokesmen. Disparate answers can readily confuse or distort the analyst's picture of the company. Beyond this, it is quite possible for a clever analyst to obtain information that the company does not want him to have by playing off one executive's statements against another's.

THE FINANCIAL RELATIONS SPECIALIST

A relative newcomer to the financial community is the financial relations specialist, whose main function is to deal with security analysts. Such men are sometimes found on the staffs of larger corporations, but most companies use the services of specialists attached to financial relations consulting firms.

Qualifications. The problem of selecting outside consultants is considered in detail in the previous chapter. For the present purpose, it is sufficient to say that the financial relations specialist should be:

1. *Headquartered in New York,* the heart of the financial community. Hiring an outside consultant based in another city is tantamount to fighting a fire raging in Oklahoma City from Los Angeles.

2. *A full-time consultant,* not a friend who is a security analyst or a helpful registered representative with extra time on his

hands. The role of financial relations specialist is much too important to entrust to someone on a part-time basis.

3. *Experienced in financial work,* preferably as a security analyst, investment adviser, or investment banker. Consultants with a newspaper or public-relations background may do a good job with news media but rarely have the financial expertise to talk on the analyst's level.

Role.   A qualified specialist can serve several functions. He can be used for:

1. *Arranging meetings* between company executives and security analysts.

2. *Meeting with analysts* himself to inform them of, and interest them in, the company's progress.

3. *Supplying information* needed by the analyst to save the time of key executives.

4. *Answering follow-up questions* after the analyst's visit to the company. Analysts are often reluctant to bother the president or treasurer days after the interview with a handful of forgotten but important questions, but they have no hesitancy in calling the specialist as often as necessary, knowing that working with analysts is an important part of his job.

5. *Evaluating analysts and their firms.* Some brokerage houses should be given the red-carpet treatment. Others should be handled politely or kept at a distance. This is because the research reports of some organizations command a good deal of respect; those from houses with a poor reputation can do harm through "guilt by association." When requested, the specialist can recommend which analysts should be given interviews and even how much time should be allotted them.

6. *Compiling and servicing mailing lists,* and preparing material for distribution.

Authority.   The best qualified and most efficient financial relations specialist cannot function properly unless the company's chief executive delegates to him the necessary authority. He must be given complete information, allowed ready access to all executives, and in general treated as a top company spokesman. On the other hand, if the specialist is unwilling to accept the responsibilities of a true official spokesman and does not speak frankly about corporate matters within his sphere of authority, he will be no asset to the company retaining him.

ADDRESSING SECURITY ANALYST SOCIETIES

The factors affecting the decision to accept an invitation to address an analysts' meeting are discussed below (see page 131). Once the invitation is accepted, however, it is usually clear that the occasion is important enough for the chief executive to be the principal speaker. Some of the largest corporations receive so many invitations of this kind that they are constantly faced with the choice of refusing the invitation or having some other spokesman address the group. Although many smaller, regional societies will accept divisional and staff executives as representatives of the company, a group will generally prefer to reject a substitute and invite the president for a more convenient date.

These meetings are no longer nearly as demanding as they once were. Everyone is polite. Few embarrassing questions are asked. However, since a large group of analysts is being addressed en masse and the press may be present, it is well for the speaker to be even more careful in choosing his words and subject matter than if he were talking to one analyst alone in his office.

Assuming that the president is a good speaker, it is best that he be the only speaker, although other executives can profitably participate in answering questions that fall in their own special province. If the president is not a good speaker, he should still give the principal address, though he may rely more heavily on others throughout the meeting. His deficiencies can be partially overcome by using well-conceived visual aids and inviting brief discussions of particular areas of the business by other members of the executive staff.

WHAT TO TELL THE ANALYST

The better the investing public understands a company the better it is able to appraise that company. The degree to which a company is understood by the investing public depends, to a great extent, on the professional security analyst, since the security analyst provides a major link between a company and investors.

It is the analyst's main function to assess a company's profit potential. To do so, he must understand a company's background, progress, policies, plans, and potential.

It is the function of the company to make sure that the analyst is as informed as possible. The attitude of the company ought to be open, helpful, and affirmative, rather than secretive, reluctant, and defensive. The company should initiate getting information to the analyst rather than passively waiting for the analyst to ask for information.

Bounded only by the need to keep some inner matters confidential, a company should be prepared to provide an analyst with all the factual and most of the subjective information he requests. One simple but basic guide is that a company ought to keep an analyst so well informed about its activities that he is never surprised when the company's quarterly sales and earnings figures are ultimately released.

INFORMATION NEEDED BY THE ANALYST

Sales and Earnings Forecasts.   It is the security analyst's job —and his success is one of the bases on which his ability is evaluated—to make accurate predictions of a company's sales and earnings for the current and coming years. He rightfully expects the company to provide him with estimates made to the best of its ability and to revise them as necessary. Companies whose business is cyclical in nature can be expected to make forecasts accurate only to the extent that they allow a sufficient range between high and low figures to accommodate the variables. Companies whose business is relatively steady over time should be able to confine realistic estimates within a much narrower range.

The analyst further knows from experience that a company's estimate in January of that new year's eventual sales and earnings totals cannot possibly be as accurate as the same company's estimate made some eight months later in September. Consequently, no analyst expects an executive to pinpoint earnings 12 months in advance. In fact, an executive who does crawl out on such a long, thin limb is performing a disservice by leading the analyst to believe he, the executive, can come up with exact estimates.

But an analyst does expect an executive to narrow the range of his earnings estimates as he approaches the close of the calendar or fiscal year, and at year's end—but before the final audit has been completed—there is little reason for an executive not to put those estimates within a fairly close range.

Since the well-managed company must forecast income as a basis for preparing operating budgets, the executive cannot protect himself from the danger of giving out faulty predictions by saying that the company makes no estimates. The analyst understands that projections of sales and earnings can be wrong and may have to be revised, but he probably cannot be convinced that they do not exist.

Corporate Policy. The most carefully constructed estimates of future sales and earnings and all the statistics available are still insufficient to give the analyst the kind of insight necessary for an accurate judgment of the company's profit potential. He must understand how the company chooses to conduct itself, the policies that serve to lead or hinder a company in its quest for profits. Although this would appear to be obvious to enlightened management, analysts complain that they are often kept completely in the dark about important corporate policies.

A consequence of not keeping analysts informed about policy decisions can be seen in the case of a Michigan manufacturer of earth-moving equipment. Operating under an openly announced policy of diversification, the manufacturer acquired within four years three companies in totally unrelated fields. At that point, the company changed the policy: Henceforth, it would acquire only companies in fields in which it was then operating. For reasons unknown it neglected to announce its change in attitude. As a result the security analysts did not spot the change until two more companies had been acquired. During the months when the company should have been talking about its plans to penetrate deeper into existing markets, analysts were waiting to see what new excursions the company would make into unexplored fields. No serious harm was done. The company merely missed an opportunity to strengthen itself in the eyes of the financial community.

While corporate policies and management's sales and earnings expectations are the analyst's prime concerns, he needs to know a number of other things about various aspects of the business in order to do his job properly. Some of the more important subjects about which analysts need information are tabulated in Fig. 10–1.

Subject Area	Matters of Policy	Miscellaneous
Acquisitions	Are acquisitions sought? If so, are they for diversification only, for greater control of one market, or to complement existing strengths?	What are the details of an accomplished acquisition, such as price (stock, cash, or both) and terms of payment? What are sales and earnings of acquired company? How will new company fit into present operations?
Advertising	How does the company determine its advertising budget? Length of time a new product will be subsidized by a high advertising-to-sales ratio?	What is the company's advertising budget? Yearly? By broad product categories? What audience is the company trying to reach? What media are used to reach audiences? Amount spent by broad product classifications? Amount company will spend to introduce a new product? Why did the company change advertising agencies?
Backlog		What is the company's backlog position? Size today? Today's size relative to past backlogs? Amount of backlog to be shipped in current year? Orders taken that may provide unusual profits

Fig. 10–1. Questions of Analysts, by Subject Area

Subject Area	Matters of Policy	Miscellaneous
		or losses? Amount of backlog subject to customer cancellation?
Capital Expenditures		What is the company's capital budget? Volume of past expenditures? Anticipated projects— short term and long term? How will they be financed? Depreciation policies?
Dependence on External Factors		Is the business dependent on factors outside its influence such as new construction activity, the high-school population, or new car sales?
Dividends	Attitude toward percentage of earnings paid as dividends, stock dividends, and stock splits?	
Financial Reports, Unusual Items		Do the financial statements include any non-recurring items? Is there any capitalization of items such as R&D costs, new product development expenses, or moving and opening expenses of a new plant?
Financing	Attitude towards debt, common stock, preferred stock, convertible securities, leases or sale-leaseback arrangements, and temporary dilution of per-share earnings? What debt-equity ratio does the company seek? What return on investment does the company want before it will allocate capital funds?	
Foreign Operations	Attitude toward manufacturing abroad vs. exporting from U.S.? Does or will company duplicate total domestic product line or	Consolidated? Unconsolidated? Influence of foreign exchanges? Breakdown of foreign sales and earnings by region? Importance of any one country?

Fig. 10–1. (Continued)

Subject Area	Matters of Policy	Miscellaneous
	make a limited penetration? Does company prefer partial ownership by local citizens, joint ventures, wholly owned operations financed by p a r e n t, management contracts, or other?	
Government Contracts	Percentage of governmental sales company would like to maintain? Policy on cost-plus contracts?	Amount of direct sales to government? Indirect sales? Names of government agencies and prime contractors sold to? Major projects?
Income Taxes		Any variance between normal rate and rate company pays? Between one year's tax rate and previous year's?
Labor		Details of company's labor contracts? Which unions represent employees? Any contractual increased labor costs soon coming up? When do contracts expire? Any strike threats in offing? History of labor relations? Ability to attract good labor for future needs?
Management	Is management centralized with most decisions made at top? Is it decentralized with divisional executives having substantial freedom? What investment return is demanded of managers? Are sufficient personnel being developed from within? Are incentives sufficient to get and keep high-caliber individuals?	
New Products	Emphasis on developing new products internally? Reliance on acquisitions for "new"	

Fig. 10–1. (Continued)

Subject Area	Matters of Policy	Miscellaneous
	products? Will company market entirely unrelated products? Will it try to develop new brand names? Will it introduce a product similar to one sold by competition?	
Patent Protection		How long does protection last? How important is it? What percentage of sales and earnings are protected by patents?
Pension Fund		What are pension fund costs? How are contributions determined? Any departures from past handling? Effect on earnings from year to year?
Profits		What is breakdown of profits by principal product areas or divisions?
Raw Materials	What is normal inventory position? Size of inventory position company will take when there is possibility of strike by major supplier? Will company hedge positions to guard against price swings when important raw material is a widely fluctuating commodity?	Is company heavily dependent on certain raw materials? What are they? Any changes anticipated in selling prices of these items? What has their price history been?
Research	To which area are research efforts directed? Other fields of interest in the future? How are research expenditures calculated?	How much is spent on research? What costs go into research budget? How effective have past corporate research expenditures been? What new products have been developed in past five years? What percentage do those new products contribute to current sales and earnings?
Sales		What are sources of sales? What are sales breakdowns by principal products or divisions?

Fig. 10–1. (Continued)

WHAT NOT TO TELL THE ANALYST

Competitive Secrets.   Not even the most inquisitive analyst expects the company to reveal competitive secrets to him. He understands that profit margins on individual products are top secret. He appreciates the fact that the company will no more reveal its future marketing strategies than a general would disclose which hill he planned to attack next.

However, the analyst would not be a good analyst if he always tried to see things from the company's point of view and automatically censored himself whenever he doubted the propriety of a particular question. Thus, in the course of discussions with management, the analyst may ask a question that can be answered only by divulging information that might help competition, such as "How much advertising are you budgeting for the introduction of your new ABC product?" If the company thinks it will hurt its marketing position by revealing this information in advance, it should withhold the answer—not make a vague reply designed to dodge the question—and tell the analyst why.

The analyst may choose not to pursue the subject or he may try to get the answer in a roundabout way. He may ask, "What will be the initial advertising-to-sales ratio?" and sometime later in the discussion, "What kind of volume do you anticipate the first year?"

It is easy for the executive being interviewed to give partial answers to seemingly innocent followup questions, but it is extremely unwise. If a little information is given, the door is open for further probing. It is best to answer all queries touching a taboo subject by firmly stating that the information cannot be revealed.

ARE THEY SECRETS?   It should be kept in mind that disclosure to analysts of valuable intelligence about the company's competitive position is not a frequent problem. On the contrary, executives generally talk less than they should about what they believe are "competitive secrets" because they refuse to credit competitors with an equal degree of intelligence.

It is usually safe to assume that Company A's competitor knows *at least* as much about Company A as Company A knows about the competitor. Competitive intelligence circulates in many ways. When, for example, Company A's competitor conducts a retail-movement survey of its own products, it will collect data on shelf turnover of Company A's products as well.

Any president who doubts the scope of such competitive intelligence need only ask his own management team to report to him everything it knows about its major competitor. The data he will receive will be staggering.

Keeping information from the analyst that is already known to the competition cannot help the company and its stockholders and may harm them by restricting the background information needed by the analyst to evaluate the company's situation properly. In some instances, when discussing such competitive information, it may be possible to satisfy the analyst's needs without being so precise as to damage the company's position— the executive being interviewed need not always quote figures to the last decimal place. If asked what sales amounted to for a certain segment of the business, and he has a good idea of the competitor's comparable sales totals, he can, if this is desirable, provide approximations that are adequate for the analyst's purposes, such as, "Sales of product line X were in the neighborhood of $15 to $17 million last year" or "Product Y accounted for roughly 20% of sales."

Other Confidential Information. Pending mergers, acquisitions under consideration, stock splits, changes in dividend policy, and other moves apt to have a decided effect on the price action of a company's stock should never be discussed with individual analysts until they are announced to the public at large.

It may seem superfluous to warn the company executive against discussing such matters prematurely and "off the record" with the analyst. However, this happens with sufficient frequency to warrant some emphasis on the dangers involved.

Unless management is ready to tell the world, it should not tell the analyst. There are two principal reasons why secrets told off the record often go beyond the analyst to others in the financial community:

First, analysts from different firms specializing in a common industry frequently discuss their mutual interest in a company. During such talks, the analyst can hardly be expected to remember in every instance what he was told off the record, nor can he be expected to consult his notes—where, it is hoped, he wrote "off the record" in the margin—every time a particular company is brought into the discussion.

Second, in some firms it is the practice for analysts to file their notes where others in a research department can easily— and ethically—read them. Consequently, the analyst has little control over the security of confidential information given him by company executives.

Although many executives will not talk off the record with "ordinary" analysts from brokerage firms, they may feel safe in discussing confidential material with analysts from the research departments of institutions interested only in their own portfolios and not motivated to publish market letters or research reports. In addition to the impropriety of telling one analyst something that is withheld from another, there is also the danger that it is quite possible for a friendly institutional analyst who has been given corporate secrets to find himself suddenly in a new job with a brokerage house where those secrets may find their way into a research report.

HOW NOT TO MISLEAD THE ANALYST

Every discussion with a security analyst should be as objective and factual as possible. In this connection, there are three major errors made by company executives in giving information to analysts.

Overconservative Estimates.   While it is quite natural to pursue a conservative approach in dealing with security analysts, a company executive has no right to give out estimates of earnings substantially lower than he actually anticipates. If he does, he is in fact misleading the investment public and is not being conservative in the true sense of the word. For example, if a company earned $2.25 per share last year and expects to earn $3 this year, the spokesman cannot rightly say that earnings this year will be slightly better. A 33⅓ per cent increase in earnings is substantially better than "slight."

The stockholder in a company that did not inform the investing public that earnings would show a substantial earnings increase can, through premature sale of his stock, lose just as much money and feel just as cheated as the investor who purchased stock on the basis of a highly inflated earnings estimate. Stockholders who did not increase their holdings and potential investors who decided not to buy stock because they interpreted deliberately deflated earnings estimates literally also have grounds for indignation.

Executives have a duty to give earnings and sales estimates that truly represent their thinking.

Overoptimistic Estimates. While an understatement of estimated earnings is usually deliberate, overoptimistic estimates most often result from management's honest enthusiasm brought on by a new product, a new plant, or some other promising development.

To say that such enthusiasm can backfire is to state the obvious. New products can and do fizzle in the market place despite an excellent showing in test markets. New equipment can require a longer break-in period or new processes can develop bugs that take far more time and money to eliminate than could have been foreseen. Two examples follow:

The earnings of a Midwestern manufacturing company increased from $1.01 to $1.16 to $1.35 per share in the three years preceding the construction of a new major plant. The company proudly announced to its stockholders that although the move into the plant would cost the company about 20 cents a share, general business improvements would still make possible a further slight increase in earnings for the fourth year. Actually, the moving cost was expected to be 16 cents per share, but the company president was providing himself with a 4-cent safety-margin allowance. The plant was occupied not too far behind schedule, but the cost of making the move was almost four times that anticipated. Earnings per share for the fourth year slumped to $.78. This is not an unusual case. Any company that has not been involved with a major plant move within the past decade is likely to seriously underestimate the costs involved.

An Eastern seaboard company reported to stockholders that the economies resulting from a new acquisition would almost double earnings in the following year. However, the initial costs of combining the new and old operations turned out to be so much greater than anticipated that earnings actually dropped 30 per cent.

In talks with security analysts, the wise executive tempers with caution his enthusiasm about promising circumstances.

Hiding Information.   Some executives conceal any disagreeable facts about their company, perhaps in some instances in the belief that bad news reflects on their own personal abilities. Such secrecy, unwise at best, can in the long run lead to rumors far more harmful to the company than the truth. The experience of a Chicago manufacturer provides an excellent example:

One of the company's important divisions suddenly went into a sales slump in January, a peak month. By early April the division's sales were off 9 per cent, but the decline seemed to be leveling off. The several analysts who visited the company during January, February, and March were not told about the problem, and when company-wide quarterly figures were released they did not spot the slump because sales in other divisions were up somewhat over the preceding year.

By the end of April, Wall Street had somehow gotten wind of the ailing division—perhaps through indiscreet marketing or sales personnel, competitors' market research data, or analysts' interviews with retail sales employees. Immediately, the rumor mills went to work. It was said that the trouble would drag total corporate earnings down by the end of the year, that it was a symptom of a serious top-management problem, that the company was considering selling the division.

By July the company's stock was off 20 per cent despite the fact that total sales were up 5 per cent for the first half-year. The sales problem was solved before the end of the year, but the price-earnings ratio of the company's stock took several years to return to its previous level.

The company president never did explain the division's problem to the financial community. Early in the year he should have told analysts: "We have a sales problem in the XYZ Division. Right now sales are off 9 per cent from last year. Here's what we're doing to correct the situation. This is how long it should take for the change to be felt." Analysts will treat adversity realistically once they are told what the company is doing to overcome it.

Another and more sensitive situation demanding full and immediate disclosure is declining profits. The company should make certain that the lowered earnings estimate reported to analysts will not have to be reduced again later.

By candidly discussing difficulties, the company can gain the analyst's confidence and support, and through him that of the entire financial community.

MEETINGS WITH GROUPS

If a publicly owned company needed to communicate with security analysts only when it was announcing a development of major news interest, the easiest way would be to mail an announcement to all security analysts who follow the company. However, a company has much more information to impart to security analysts than quarterly earnings reports and the half-dozen or so news stories that arise each year. For this reason, companies (1) invite security analysts to company-sponsored meetings, (2) send their top executives to meetings sponsored by analysts' groups, (3) participate in industry seminars, and (4) arrange field trips and plant tours for analysts. In addition, there also are occasions when executives come into direct contact with security analysts on an individual basis. The direct contact may range from a simple telephone call from an analyst asking a question to a personal interview lasting several hours. Such meetings—both with groups and with individuals—give managements an opportunity to talk about their corporations as personalities rather than as collections of statistics.

According to one estimate, publicly owned companies make well over 5,000 presentations to analyst groups each year. However, holding many meetings with analysts is obviously less important than holding the proper type of meeting.

As the research departments of brokerage firms and investment institutions have expanded, the characteristics of various security analyst groups have undergone a change. Groups that formerly were important for executives to address have diminished in significance. Others have developed to take their place. The purpose of the following discussion is to provide a guide to the selection of the proper setting—whether a group meeting or individual conversation—for communicating with security analysts on a personal basis. This is an important determinant of how effectively a company will get its story across to analysts.

Informal Talks.   A company sponsored, informal get-together with eight to ten security analysts—usually, but not necessarily, over lunch—is the best way for management to communicate *non-news* developments to the investment community. Formal speeches are not in order here. Instead, there is just an exchange of ideas between the attending analysts and the company's management.

The informal-group approach has many of the same characteristics of a personal interview, yet allows executives to talk to several analysts in almost the same time that would be spent talking with one analyst. An executive can say at least as much to a small group of analysts as he would have said to one analyst alone. It is possible that more will be said to a group simply because the members of a small group will spark each other's questions. Thus, informal meetings help analysts probe deeply —to both their benefit and management's.

Small, informal sessions designed to permit an analyst to probe are far superior to the formal analysts' session where a prepared text is delivered by a chief executive officer. Analysts much prefer the smaller group meeting.

A company can make its meetings more effective—and can more easily accomplish its own goals—by inviting at one time only analysts with similar characteristics. While it is true that security analysts in general want much the same kind of information—irrespective of whether they work for a brokerage house or an institution—there are also shades of difference in the information that analysts representing different types of firms seek to obtain. Thus, the structure of these small meetings should be tailored to suit the analysts' requirements and the company's objectives. For example, a company may choose to invite to one meeting only analysts who work in the research departments of institutions. The next time, it may hold a meeting for analysts employed by brokerage houses with many branch offices throughout the country. Still other meetings can be held with analysts of brokerage firms that deal primarily with institutions. The variations are many. Management need only determine which groups it is trying to reach.

Since the informal meeting is such a potent communications tool, a company's main efforts should be concentrated in this area. Such get-togethers should be held at frequent intervals and on a regular basis—regardless of whether the company's operations look favorable or unfavorable. When possible, these informal meetings should be held in various cities to help the company achieve geographic diversity among its stockholders.

One word of caution: Management should not make a news announcement to an informal group. News announcements should be issued to the general public. Small meetings are for discussions of the company's activities and plans.

Security Analysts' Societies. NEW YORK SOCIETY OF SECURITY ANALYSTS. By all yardsticks, The New York Society of Security Analysts is the largest, most important, and most influential of the formal security analyst groups a company can address. Inherent in this group, however, are certain drawbacks. Executives ought to be aware of them.

A talk before the N.Y.S.S.A. is no longer as vital as it once was. Years ago when the N.Y.S.S.A. was an important forum whose invitation no company could afford to ignore, any chief executive officer then addressing the group was bombarded with searching questions that often put him on the spot. The resulting answers gave those analysts an intimate knowledge of the company and its objectives. But as the N.Y.S.S.A. grew bigger, its meetings lost their zest: speeches became more formal; questions grew less discerning, answers more general. Despite attempts to improve these daily N.Y.S.S.A. meetings, analysts attending them today rarely get enough information to enable them to make an adequate appraisal of a company's present situation.

In addition, executives addressing the N.Y.S.S.A. are frequently unable to communicate with the audience they need to reach. Such is the case when a senior analyst—one who has the greatest reponsibility for following the company—sends an assistant to the meeting because he, the senior man, has a more pressing engagement and knows he can read the speech later. Here management, obviously, misses out on a face-to-face encounter with an important individual on Wall Street.

A talk before the N.Y.S.S.A. will benefit any company that wants to communicate with as many influential analysts as possible *at one time.* Such a forum is excellent when, as one example, a company lists on the New York Stock Exchange and management wants the entire investment community to get to know rapidly more about the company.

REGIONAL ANALYST SOCIETIES.   It is difficult for a company to get its story across at regional society meetings because the analysts attending are "generalists" for the most part, not industry specialists. Consequently, most regional analysts do not develop a subsequent continuing interest in any company that happens to be addressing the group.

Some companies, however, can profit to a degree by speaking before regional groups. Typically, these are local in their spheres of operation, product distribution, or services performed and therefore have strong regional ties. Appearing before its regional society helps such a company communicate with its local stockholders and also creates community goodwill by helping support the regional society, which will be relatively dependent upon interesting programs to keep up its membership (for a list of regional analyst societies that are members of The Financial Analysts Federation, see Fig. 10–2).

Atlanta Society of Financial Analysts
The Austin-San Antonio Society of Financial Analysts
The Baltimore Security Analysts Society
The Boston Security Analysts Society
The Investment Analysts Society of Chicago
The Cincinnati Society of Financial Analysts
The Cleveland Society of Security Analysts
The Columbus Society of Financial Analysts
The Dallas Association of Investment Analysts
Denver Society of Security Analysts
The Financial Analysts Society of Detroit
The Hartford Society of Financial Analysts
The Houston Society of Financial Analysts
The Indianapolis Society of Financial Analysts
The Financial Analysts Society of Jacksonville
Kansas City Society of Financial Analysts
The Los Angeles Society of Financial Analysts
Milwaukee Investment Analysts
Montreal Society of Financial Analysts
Nashville Society of Financial Analysts, Inc.

Financial Analysts of New Orleans
The New York Society of Security Analysts, Inc.
The Oklahoma Society of Financial Analysts
The Omaha-Lincoln Society of Financial Analysts
Financial Analysts of Philadelphia
Phoenix Society of Financial Analysts
Pittsburgh Society of Financial Analysts
The Providence Society of Financial Analysts
The Richmond Society of Financial Analysts
The Rochester Society of Investment Analysts
The St. Louis Society of Financial Analysts
Financial Analysts Society of San Diego
The Security Analysts of San Francisco
Financial Analysts of Toledo
The Toronto Society of Financial Analysts
The Twin Cities Society of Security Analysts, Inc.
The Washington Society of Investment Analysts
Financial Analysts of Wilmington
The Winnipeg Society of Financial Analysts

Fig. 10–2. Financial Analysts Federation Regional Societies

Copies of an executive's speech delivered to a formal analyst's group should be printed for those attending. The text can be given out at the end of the meeting or sent to analysts later with the questions and answers at the end of the speech included. However, the text should not be given out before the talk. Some analysts would spend more time flipping through the pages of the speech than in listening to it.

Specialized Security Analyst Groups. Security analysts themselves have recognized the problems created by the growth of the formal security analyst societies and the resulting loss of the personal give-and-take that previously occurred between analysts and company executives. As a result, new analysts' groups, mainly offshoots of the formal societies, have been formed to fill the void created when the latter's meetings changed in character. These specialized groups devote themselves to a specific industry; their membership, usually limited to 20 or 30, consists of those analysts who are the most knowledgeable about their field. Such men closely follow their industry's trends and the progress of the companies making it up.

Since the analysts belonging to these groups are cream-of-the-crop specialists, they play a most important role in determining the investment community's attitude toward a company. Corporate executives invited to appear before such an industry meeting should consider it a major opportunity to communicate effectively and directly with Wall Street.

These small groups meet about once a month. Typical of those formed by leading security analysts in their fields are the ones dealing with the following industries:

Paper	Utilities
Steel	Transportation
Aerospace	Entertainment
Electronics	Motor carrier
Chemicals	

Seminars and Field Trips. Some security analyst societies conduct special seminars devoted to a discussion of an entire industry. Representatives from a few of the larger companies in that industry are usually invited to participate. The purpose of the seminar is to give the analysts present a clearer understanding of the industry. Thus, the talks are *not* concerned with any individual company's activities—except as an illustration of a particular point that an executive makes while talking about the industry.

These are generally excellent gatherings for companies to participate in because they attract the analysts most interested in the industry. Although a company *per se* is not discussed, explanations of the industry by the company's executives help the company indirectly. The better the analysts understand the industry the better they will be able to evaluate each company's progress within that industry. And the seminar does give the analysts another opportunity to appraise a company executive while he is talking. If a company's executives—or its financial relations counsel—maintain a close relationship with Wall Street, they will be alerted well in advance that their industry is to be the subject of an analysts' seminar. It is perfectly acceptable to call or write to the chairman of the seminar, expressing a desire to have a representative participate.

Occasionally, a company can sponsor its own industry seminar. This gives the company an opportunity to explain its own operations while detailing the complexities of the industry as a whole. For example, Texas Eastern Transmission Corporation sponsors an annual *Natural Gas Industry Seminar* to which it invites about 30 analysts representing top investment firms, insurance companies, foundations, mutual funds and banks. The seminar, which lasts several days, is devoted to various aspects of the industry and of Texas Eastern.

While such meetings can prove helpful, they should be used as a supplement to—not as a substitute for—the private meeting that centers almost exclusively around the company's activities.

The Financial Analysts Federation conducts a convention and a field trip in a different major city each year. The Federation invites companies located in the convention-city's area to send representatives to address specialized industry groups. Frequently, plant tours (see below) are arranged for analysts attending. Since the schedule for these convention-field trips is available several years in advance, companies conveniently located at the site of an upcoming meeting can write the Federation's Program Committee, asking to be included in that meeting.

Brokerage Firm Meetings.   Some brokerage firms hold meetings that allow company executives to address the brokerage firm's own personnel. In addition to members of the research department, registered representatives are invited to these sessions.

A number of brokerage houses frequently hold meetings—usually at lunch—to bring together the executives of one company and some 20 to 35 security analysts representing institutional investors. That way an important group of analysts either becomes acquainted with a company they previously knew little about or is brought up to date with the current operations and plans of a company they have been following. Apart from the commission business that may be generated for the sponsoring brokerage house, the broker arranges these meetings to perform a two-fold service: for the institution, such a meeting provides a convenient opportunity to obtain first-hand knowledge of a company in which it may have an interest; for the company, the meeting provides an opportunity to present its story before an influential group.

Plant Tours.   Plant tours are effective from the analyst's point of view only (1) when a company has something to show that will further his knowledge in an area that he deems important or (2) when a company's operations are such that only actually seeing the operation will impart a full understanding of what is being accomplished. If neither of these conditions is met, a plant tour should *not* be held. Most analysts have visited so many plants in their careers that by now most plants look alike to them. Executives should not confuse their own pride in a major capital addition with something sufficiently unique to justify the time an analyst must devote to a plant tour.

When a tour is appropriate, it should be conducted for selected groups of interested analysts. Enough time should be given after the tour for analysts to interview management on the financial aspects of what was shown to them during the tour.

What the Analysts Want To Hear. No matter how intimate or prestigious the group addressed, the speech must have the right content and presentation to be of any value. If the executive offers warmed-over information to the analysts and compounds the error by presenting the rehash in a routine fashion, he will undoubtedly stir up resentment against the company among the analysts, turning a potentially beneficial session into a harmful one.

Unfortunately, that is the approach taken by far too many executives today, according to many analysts. Too few companies, these analysts complain, are providing the beneath-the-surface information they need to make investment recommendations. The analysts' biggest complaint: the speeches are deadly dull. Specifically, the things that irk the analysts are: too much company history, not enough information on research and development; and not enough hard facts on markets and sales projections.

The Investment Analysts Society of Chicago sends a brochure to its invited speakers to let them know what the Society expects to hear. Among the instructions spelled out in that brochure is this relevant piece of advice:

Please bear in mind that members of the Society are assumed to be reasonably well acquainted with your company's history and recent events which have been reported publicly. We particularly urge that your remarks concern present and future prospects, including comments on such items as new products under development, trends in the industry, projections of capital expenditures, financing requirements, the regulatory outlook if applicable, the competitive situation, and rates of production.

To liven up a speech—and at the same time improve communication—visual aids are helpful. Charts, graphs, films, and product display all enable an analyst to get a clearer picture of what the company executive is saying. And that is precisely what the speaker's goal ought to be.

Moreover, a company should talk not only about itself but

about its industry as well. The economic factors that affect the industry or special considerations that make it fundamentally different from other related industries should be pointed out. Apart from making the talk more interesting, such industry information helps an analyst appraise a company far more effectively.

HANDLING ANALYSTS ON AN INDIVIDUAL BASIS

Most meetings with groups of analysts are company initiated. However, there are many times when a face-to-face (or telephone-to-telephone) encounter with a security analyst occurs because the analyst—not the company—has taken the initiative. At such times, the analyst (or analysts) may be calling for a clarification: earnings are up but the profit margin is down, and he would like to know the reason. Or, the analyst on the telephone wants a personal interview with the president.

Allotting Time to Analysts.   An executive's time is a critical factor in dealing on a personal basis with security analysts. For an idea of the amount of time devoted each year to interviews with analysts, consider the estimates made by the presidents of the following corporations: Sinclair Oil Corporation —more than 100 hours; Amsted Industries, Inc.—one or two interviews each week averaging an hour and a half each; Worthington Corporation—six to eight interviews a month averaging two to three hours apiece; and the Standard Oil Company (Ohio)—75 to 100 hours a year.

Executives of a company with investment popularity obviously cannot please every analyst who knows the company's telephone number. Actually, not all analysts ought to be given equal time. Certain brokerage houses are more influential in determining attitudes of the investment community towards the company than are others and the analysts from such brokerage houses should be given more time. The same rule applies to analysts from investment institutions that command a great deal of respect from the investment community. Or the knowledge or capability of a particular analyst may warrant devoting extra time to him.

At the other extreme, there are some brokerage houses with such poor reputations that a company would be better off not having that firm recommend the company's stock. In such cases, the company should try to avoid—or at least severely limit—interviews with analysts. There are also analysts— perhaps with good firms—who are of such poor caliber that they should be discouraged from taking up executive time with personal interviews. These analysts do not bother to do any research before coming to the meeting; or they try to tell company executives how to run their business; or they try to sell something—say, their firms qualifications as the source of the company's next financing—under the guise of doing security research.

There are countless brokerage houses that are neither outstanding nor bad, employing relatively competent analysts. When possible, executives should try to combine requests for personal interviews from such firms so that a group of those analysts will meet with the chief executive officer at one time.

While the time allotted to analysts will vary depending on their reputation or that of the company they represent, every analyst should receive a similar response to the same questions, and information should not be withheld from one that is given to another. The difference, then, hinges not on what is told to analysts but, primarily, on how discerning the analysts' questions are and, secondarily, on how much time is given to each analyst to ask his questions.

Individual Meetings. Face-to-face meetings between analysts and top management can get out of hand if not properly conducted. Among the things management should do to get the best results from a personal interview, two are of primary importance:

PREPARE ANALYST FOR MEETING. To rid the meeting of a lot of questions about things the analyst should have known before the interview ("Do you have a stock option plan?" "In which cities are your plants located?" "What are the names of the unions representing your employees?") management should send the analyst all pertinent published information in advance of the interview. The analyst then has no excuse for not having done his homework.

SET TIME LIMIT ON MEETING. Depending on the personality of the analyst, an interview can be concise and to the point or it can ramble on and on for hours. To avoid an unduly prolonged meeting, it is perfectly permissible when setting up the date to ask the analyst how much time he will need. If the amount of time he requests is deemed reasonable, he should be granted that time—with the understanding that that will be all he will get. Such limitations force him to keep to the point. Naturally, if the meeting is going well and the executive wishes to continue longer, he may do so.

To terminate the interview at the proper time, it is wise to alert the analyst to the time remaining some ten or fifteen minutes before the deadline. He then has the opportunity to ask whatever important questions are still in his mind. Without such a warning, the analyst may leave feeling frustrated because he did not get to ask what he considered to be the most important questions. In addition, a subtle time warning sets the stage for the termination of the interview.

Telephone Calls. Analysts' telephone calls for information generally follow one of two patterns. Each should be dealt with differently.

CALLS CONCERNED WITH IMMEDIATE NEWS. Since these telephone calls are stimulated by specific events, they tend to come in bunches and are difficult to space out. A call of this nature usually occurs as a reaction to (1) a sudden move in the price of a stock, either up or down, (2) unusual volume in the stock, (3) a rumor, (4) a news announcement that needs further amplification, or (5) someone looking for a buyer or seller of a block of stock. Despite the disruptive nature of these calls, each should be handled promptly.

CALLS REQUESTING GENERAL INFORMATION. Such calls come from security analysts who want general information about the company's situation. They are time consuming, and executives should allow sufficient time to handle them adequately. Since there is usually no great urgency, it is perfectly proper for the executive to postpone taking the call or to tell the analyst that he will call him back at a specific time. However, these should not be mere delaying tactics; every effort should be made to free some time to talk to the analyst within a day or so.

Records of Analyst Contacts. While records concerning contacts with security analysts add to the paperwork, they are indispensable. One of their most important functions is to help management alter, if necessary, any estimate that has been given to an analyst or a group of analysts.

For example: A chief executive may have told five or six analysts that a loss division would be operating profitably by the end of the year and would not be a drain on earnings. Unfortunately, he subsequently realizes that it will take longer than anticipated to get that division in the black and as a result total company earnings will be lower than expected. How does the chief executive communicate this information to the men most vitally concerned—those who were specifically told the division would not be hurting total earnings? Without records it is an almost impossible task, but with the help of a simple card file (analyst's name and company affiliation, a condensed run-down of the estimates given to the analyst, the date of the meeting, and the way the data was communicated—telephone, in person, or in correspondence) the executive, or a member of his financial relations staff, can call each analyst and explain that the information he was originally given was incorrect and give him the reasons for the change.

Record keeping serves other functions as well. Records of analyst meetings, for example, help management—or its financial relations counsel—keep up to date on which members

of the financial community are interested in the company so
that the analysts can be supplied with additional information
as it develops.

Timing of Analysts' Recommendations.   Typically, when an
analyst is preparing a recommendation of a company's stock,
he will check with the company to see whether there are any
late developments he should know about. In this way, management is often alerted that a particular brokerage house has a
recommendation in the works. Should it be learned that several
brokerage firms are planning to recommend purchase of the
company's stock at about the same time, analysts calling subsequently to check on latest developments can be informed
that other reports are about to be issued. As a result a broker
may temporarily delay a recommendation so as not to over-
stimulate the market and cause the stock to soar above the
price at which his firm would want its customers to buy the
stock.

11

Mailings to Security Analysts

A security analyst needs to receive a regular flow of company information if he is to evaluate that company properly and keep abreast of current developments. Steady mailings of pertinent data to security analysts following the company serve these specific purposes:

1. They bring the information to the right analyst—the man who is following the company and its industry.
2. They give the analyst data in handy, easy-to-file fashion. Otherwise the analyst would have to clip a newspaper article to have the information for future reference.
3. They emphasize to the analyst what the company is doing and supply him with immediate, detailed data about a specific activity within the company.

Unfortunately, the mailing practices of many companies may—and often do—misfire for one of two basic reasons. Either a company sends the analyst too much material, inundating his desk with trivia, or it neglects the analyst, sending only the annual report and interim statements. To communicate properly with an analyst, a company must be sensitive to his needs. With these in mind, management must evaluate everything it sends to him in terms of whether it will help further his knowledge about the company or its industry in the areas where he wants his knowledge furthered. Naturally, the analyst does not want a rehash of those things he already knows.

Too frequently, management thinks of the analyst as a storehouse for all miscellaneous data. Such is far from the case. If management is not certain that the analyst needs or wants the information, it should *not* be mailed. It is better to err on the conservative side than to take the wholesale-broadcasting approach.

This chapter will discuss what to send to an analyst, what *not* to send, which analysts to send material to, and how to time mailings.

WHAT TO SEND SECURITY ANALYSTS

Routine Announcements. Most announcements to the public at large concerning the corporation—as opposed to those concerning local or divisional matters—should be sent to security analysts. To illustrate: The regular reports a company ordinarily issues to its stockholders—annual reports, proxy statements, interim sales and earnings reports, and dividend changes—should also be sent to security analysts. When possible, separate reports that include more detailed financial information and background material should be sent to the analyst in place of or as a supplement to stockholder reports.

Moreover, important news releases sent to the press—but ordinarily not to stockholders—also should be sent to analysts. Such releases include corporate announcements of: capital expenditure programs, new financing, major new product developments, and changes in selling prices.

Special Material. While material designed for others—annual reports to stockholders, press releases to newspapers—is helpful to a security analyst, special publications designed with only the analyst's needs in mind should be developed and mailed.

One excellent special publication is an "Information Report" or "Fact Book" which presents comprehensive data about a company and its industry by bringing together in a single volume the trends, statistics, background, historical data, capabilities, markets, research activities, facilities, etc., that will be of use to the analyst and further his understanding of the company's operations.

The "Fact Book" should be designed solely to provide *information* from which an analyst can draw his own conclusions. It should never be used as a promotional device. Care should be taken that there is no hint that the company is implying any recommendations of its stock or that it is slanting the report in its own favor. In the writing of the "Fact Book," words should be chosen with great care. Laudatory adjectives, for example, should be omitted. Such adjectives make the "Fact Book" a subjective document; what the analyst requires is *objectivity*.

"Fact Books" are becoming more popular as companies recognize the benefits to be derived from an objective and across-the-board financial review of the company in one compact source. Crompton & Knowles Corporation, for example, issued a 17-page "Information Study" describing the company, its capabilities, markets, research activities, acquisition program, facilities, and foreign operations. Chrysler Corporation supplied analysts with even greater detail in a 54-page "Financial and Statistical Fact Book."

Reprints of Speeches.   Many speeches given by a company's chief executive officer and directed to a financial or an investment audience will be of interest to security analysts who follow the company's industry. Other kinds of talks—nonfinancial talks—given by executives other than the chief executive officer may also be of interest to the analyst, e.g. those given by a company officer to a marketing group.

A talk given by a company officer at an industry seminar,

as another example, may warrant a mailing to security analysts —even though the talk is limited to a discussion of the industry as a whole. The president of one medium-size telephone company delivered a speech on "Independent Telephone Technical Advances" without ever mentioning his company in the talk. The reprint of that speech was a valuable contribution to analysts in that it enabled them to achieve a deeper understanding of the independent telephone industry and, hence, of the company itself.

Magazine Articles. Whenever a story is published that affords a good insight into a company, a reprint of the article will be useful in helping analysts understand the company. Articles that may be of interest to analysts cover such subjects as marketing, advertising, production, research, finance, management, or acquisition programs. Union Carbide Corporation sent reprints of an article from *Sales Management Magazine* that reported in detail the company's marketing program, discussing the changing organizational structures and marketing strategies of its major operating divisions.

In addition to magazine articles about the company, analysts also welcome well-researched magazine articles that explain the forces at work in an industry or give background material about factors that may influence the industry's future. Such articles can be of great assistance to an analyst. Even when a company is not mentioned in such an industry review, an analyst will appreciate the service rendered by the company in providing a reprint. Thus, any company sending out a reprint of an industry story gets two benefits: the analyst will get a better understanding of the company via his better understanding of the industry; and the company will gain his good will for its service to the financial community.

When the Taylor Wine Company fills requests for information about the company, it includes a reprint of a magazine article that describes the making and marketing of wine in the Finger Lakes region of New York State, together with background information on the industry. A major producer of New York State wines, Taylor helps the analyst learn more about the specific segment of the industry in which it operates.

News Summaries. Companies with many divisions and subsidiaries often have a constant stream of news emanating from the various segments of the organization. However, since much of this information is not of an overall corporate nature —nor of timely importance—it should *not* be sent to analysts when issued to the press. Periodically, however, several pages of capsule one-paragraph summaries may be sent. Naturally, only the most important information should be included.

Some large companies issue monthly news digests prepared especially for financial analysts, which may include upwards of 15 or 20 items covering topics that range from foreign market activities to new-product developments. The monthly digest provides a quick way for the analyst to keep abreast of a company's activities. If news releases on each subject were sent to the analyst, they would swamp him.

Advertisement Reprints and Samples. Apart from what has already been discussed, there is yet another information area that may be of value to an analyst. The best way to explain what falls into this category is through two examples:

When a company embarks on a new direction in its advertising strategy, a mailing to the analyst of the new series of advertisements may be the best demonstration of the company's changed marketing approach.

Similarly, a company about to market an important new product on a national basis may send a sample of that product to security analysts, provided the product is of nominal monetary value. A new-product mailing to the analysts often will help illustrate what the product will do much more clearly than a news announcement about the product.

Regulatory Agency Filings. Some of the filings that any company must make—with the S.E.C., I.C.C., and F.P.C., for example—may prove valuable to security analysts. Analysts welcome getting a copy of these documents for their files. Some examples:

1. *Prospectus:* When new stock is being issued or a secondary offering is being made, a company's prospectus will generally give facts and financial breakdowns not normally published.

2. *Listing statements:* When a company lists on an exchange or files to have additional shares listed, its listing statement frequently contains data not made public before.

3. *Other documents:* Although many of the documents a company must file with governmental organizations—such as 10K forms—are available for public inspection at designated offices and may be purchased, a company should make it easy for an analyst to get them. They need not be mailed as a matter of course, but copies should be supplied on request.

WHAT NOT TO SEND SECURITY ANALYSTS

If the information management plans to send an analyst does not communicate something about the company's current activities or its future prospects, or at least give background information on the company or the industry that he does not already have, then that information should *not* be mailed.

Once an analyst gets in the habit of discarding much of the material a company sends him because he cannot use it, he is likely, out of habit, to treat an important announcement in the same manner.

Most Executive Appointments. Apart from the announcement of the election of a new chief executive officer—which is news an analyst wants to receive—the election of most officers or directors is usually not of any concern to the analyst. Except in certain specific instances, perhaps because of a company's individual circumstances, an executive's prominence, or a director's affiliation, the news of most executive appointments is just not sufficiently important to be mailed to an analyst.

Routine Dividend Declarations. Increases and decreases in the regular dividend, a stock dividend, and a stock split are of immediate interest to an analyst. But a *regular* dividend announcement holds little interest for him—unless there had been rumors that a change in the dividend rate was imminent. Management should not confuse the need of statistical services for information about regular dividend declarations with the needs of security analysts.

Most Reprints. Unless there is something particularly appropriate in an advertisement that will enable an analyst to learn more about the company, advertising reprints should not be mailed. In fact, analysts regard such reprints as a nuisance. For the most part, articles about a company appearing in magazines and newspapers are a rehash of information the analyst already knows. Thus, such reprints of routine information sent to an analyst merely waste his time.

Brokerage Recommendations. While a favorable research report prepared by a brokerage house may be helpful to all analysts on a company's mailing list, such reports should *not* be mailed, because there is too great a possibility that the analyst will misconstrue the company's purposes. It is possible for some analysts to get the impression that management is overly concerned with the price of its stock, and such an attitude on the part of the analyst will have a negative effect on the company's image in the financial community. Certainly, if during a personal interview with a company executive, an analyst asks which firms recently have written recommendations of the company's stock, the executive may answer the question with no fear that he may be promoting the stock. When requested, the chief executive officer may also give the analyst a copy of the report, unless the recommending brokerage house has specifically asked to have the report kept confidential.

MAILING LISTS

Not every security analyst follows every publicly owned company. Indeed, probably less than 5% of the more than 10,000 security analysts in this nation are interested in any one particular company. Management should send its announcements only to those analysts who are interested in the company. To do otherwise, to send out a broadside mailing to thousands of analysts who specialize in such diverse industries as railroads or cosmetics or banks, is to waste money, waste the time of those analysts, and give them a poor impression of the company.

The indiscriminate use of mailing lists in an effort to communicate with large numbers of security analysts has compounded the problem of the analyst deluged by unimportant mail. And as a natural consequence, many an analyst approaches his morning mail with suspicion and may throw out even pertinent mail without ever reading it.

Developing a Good Mailing List.   To make certain that its mailings to security analysts are effective, a company must compile its own mailing list. It is possible for management to rent inexpensively lists of security analysts; some companies do just that in the mistaken belief that the broader the distribution, the better the coverage. Such is not the case. There is no mailing list available on a rental basis that will ever be as good as a privately developed mailing list.

Sources from which a good custom-tailored list may be compiled include analysts' requests for information and interviews. Any security analyst who has written to the company to ask to have something sent to him is a natural candidate for the company's analyst mailing list. As each analyst interviews a company official, he should immediately be placed on the list.

Whenever a company's officers speak before a large group of analysts—such as one of the analyst societies—management should provide cards for the analysts to fill out asking to be placed on the mailing list.

The Financial Analysts Federation publishes an annual directory of its members along with the names of the industries in which each analyst specializes. Using this directory, a list of analysts following the company's industry can be compiled

Aerospace	Finance companies	Publications
Amusements	Foods	Real estate
Automobile & accessories	Foreign securities	Retail trade
Banks	Insurance	Rubber
Bonds	Investment companies	Steel
Brewing & distilling	Investment counselor	Technician (stock
Building materials	Leisure time	market)
Chemicals	Machinery	Textiles
Containers	Metals, non-ferrous	Tobacco
Drugs, cosmetics	Natural gas	Transportation
Economist	Office equipment	Utilities
Electronics & electrical	Oil	
products	Paper	

Fig. 11–1. The Financial Analysts Federation, Members' Fields of Specialty

(see Fig. 11–1 for a breakdown of the industry specialties included in this directory). The directory should be reviewed as it is issued each year to add any new analysts' names that show up as industry specialists. Even when an analyst does not have a specific interest in a company at a given time, he frequently likes to stay abreast of developments in all the companies in the industries he follows. Keeping him aware of the company's progress thereby increases the chance of getting him to develop a greater interest in the company.

If the mailing list does not include a specific individual from every brokerage house that holds more than a nominal amount of stock, management should learn the name of the analyst who follows the company at that brokerage house and add that name to its mailing list.

Institutions that own stock in a company typically do so in the name of a nominee. To find out which institutions do own the stock, management can consult the Nominee List published by the American Society of Corporate Secretaries. Since institutional investors tend to be substantial holders of stock —and many times have their own staffs of security analysts— management should ask the institution directly which analysts ought to be placed on the company's mailing list.

Keeping Lists Current. To be good, a list must be up to date. If an old list of security analysts is used, data will be sent to analysts no longer interested in the company. As a result, many times the new analyst who follows the industry will not get the information. Mailing lists of analysts go out of date quickly because research directors change the industry assignments of the analysts working under them, analysts change their jobs, and new analysts join research departments.

To keep a mailing list active, management should regularly "clean" or update the list. The best way to clean a list is to mail a stamped, return-addressed card to each analyst on the list to fill out and send back. The analyst should be asked to indicate on the card his answers to these questions:

1. Are you still interested in getting information from this company, or do you want to be taken off the mailing list?
2. Should someone in your department other than—or in addition to—yourself be placed on the mailing list?
3. Is your address correct?

An analyst list should be updated at least every 18 months. In the interim, management can keep its list relatively current by seeing to it that knowledge of any change of analyst personnel—or of an analyst's shifting industry interest—that is picked up through day-to-day contact with Wall Street is reflected in the mailing list immediately. It should also make certain that whenever a security analyst asks that an address be changed the request is complied with immediately. Combing through the annual roster of The Financial Analysts Federation to find the names of analysts who follow the company's industry will furnish new names not already on the mailing list.

TIMING

Up-to-the-minute information is worth much more to an analyst than information several days old. Therefore, management should time its mailings so that analysts get the company's announcements simultaneously with their publication in the newspapers or with their receipt by stockholders.

To illustrate: when earnings reports are released to the press on, say, a Wednesday afternoon, that news story will appear in Thursday's morning newspapers. If management also mails its announcement concerning the earnings to analysts on Wednesday, most of those analysts will receive the earnings reports in their mail on Thursday morning while reading the story in their morning newspapers. The chief advantage to such simultaneous mailings—the principal audience *plus* the analyst list—lies in the fact that analysts need all the information about a corporate development and not just the abbreviated version that most newspapers are forced to publish. The analyst needs complete data to appraise the company and also to answer the requests for more detail generated by the investing public once those investors have read the newspaper version of the company development. The timely mailing by management, obviously, gives the analyst all the data when he needs it.

12

Institutional Investors

Because institutional investors make, on balance, excellent stockholders, every publicly owned company—irrespective of size—should try to attract institutions to its stockholder roster. Contrary to popular belief, even small publicly held companies with relatively few shares available for trading can interest some institutions in taking an investment position in their securities.

Typically, executives of small and medium-sized companies willingly accept their lack of appeal to institutions because they limit their concept of institutional investors to mutual funds and closed-end investment companies. While it is true that such institutions concentrate their stock purchases on relatively few companies—most of which are blue chips— such large-scale investors constitute only a small percentage of the *total* institutional-investor population. There are less than 500 mutual funds and publicly held closed-end investment companies, but the total number of institutional investors is in the tens of thousands. The often forgotten institutions— which make up the majority—include: insurance companies, pension funds, profit-sharing funds, banks, trust companies, foundations, private investment companies, and college and

university endowments. The total holdings of these institutions
in New York Stock Exchange stocks comes close to $75 billion
—*excluding* the closed-end investment companies and the mutual funds, whose combined holdings total under $30 billion
(see Fig. 12–1 for size of holdings by various institutions).

Type of Institution	1967
Insurance companies:	
Life	$ 6.0
Non-life	8.9
Investment companies:	
Open-end	24.1
Closed-end	4.0
Non-insured pension funds:	
Corporate	30.8
Other private	1.9
State & local government	1.9
Nonprofit institutions:	
College & university endowments	4.4
Foundations	8.8
Other	6.9
Common trust funds	2.9
Mutual savings banks	0.5
TOTAL	$101.1
Market value of all NYSE-listed stock	$482.5
Estimated % held by all institutions	21.0%

Fig. 12–1. Estimated Holdings of New York Stock Exchange Listed
Stocks by Financial Institutions (in billions)

Many smaller institutions are actively interested in investing
in the medium-sized and relatively small companies, whether
listed or traded in the over-the-counter market. Thus, in terms
of the majority of publicly owned companies, getting institutional ownership becomes a matter of finding and attracting
some of the smaller institutions that are willing to invest in a
wide range of situations. This chapter will explain how management can attract such ownership.

ADVANTAGES OF INSTITUTIONAL STOCKHOLDERS

Institutional stockholders are unlike individual stockholders
in many ways. On balance, the differences work heavily in

favor of the company whose stock the institution owns. Specifically, institutional stockholder ownership brings the following benefits to a company:

Long-term Investments.   Most institutions will not actively trade in a company's stock. When a block of stock is bought by an institution, it typically stays in the portfolio for a long period. Naturally, at times an institution will turn around and sell a stock it recently purchased because of a changed investment appraisal, but even with the growth of "performance funds" in-and-out transactions are infrequent. Long-term ownership on the part of an institutional stockholder helps bring price stability for the company's stock.

Purchases Against Declining Market.   Since institutions are managed by professional investors, they are not prone to panic as an individual stockholder might be. On the contrary, since institutions are constantly seeking new areas of investment, they may be the ones to step in and buy securities when prices drop. An ability and willingness by institutions to buy against a declining market also contribute to a stock's price stability.

Tendency To Vote for Management.   Institutions can be counted on to vote for management and its proposals in almost every case. If an institution did not agree with management it would not have made an investment in the company's stock in the first place.

Source of New Capital and a Buyer of Secondaries.   An institution prefers to buy stock in large blocks rather than accumulating a position by buying 100 shares at a time. Since new financing and secondaries provide large-block opportunities, an institution that already has a position in a company's stock may increase its holdings when the opportunity presents itself. Similarly, an institution that had not owned the company's stock might be enticed into taking that first step— adding a new company to its portfolio—by the availability of a large block through an offering.

Stock Purchase as Seal of Approval. Mutual funds and closed-end investment companies publish quarterly reports of their stock transactions and their holdings to the public. The inclusion of a company in an institutional portfolio attracts the attention of other institutions, brokerage firms, and individual stockholders. The thinking on the part of the investment community is that if a respected fund has thought enough of a company to invest in its stock, then there must be something attractive about the company that should be investigated. Individual investors sometimes sidestep the investigatory stage and simply buy the stock on the strength of institutional ownership.

DISADVANTAGES OF INSTITUTIONAL STOCKHOLDERS

While benefits accrue to any company with institutional stockholders, there are a few attendant drawbacks to such ownership. However, in the main, the benefits to institutional ownership far outweigh whatever disadvantages may enter the picture.

Possibility of Badly Handled Sales. When an institution wishes to sell a large block of stock, it tries to sell all the shares at one time. If a large buyer and seller can locate each other —usually through a stock broker—the deal is quickly consummated. As a result, the market price for that stock is not upset. But if a buyer cannot be located quickly, or a mutually satisfactory price cannot be agreed upon, the institution may start offering the block to too many people or sell the securities piecemeal. The rumor that there is a large block of stock to be sold often is enough to depress its price. Steady selling day after day invariably worsens the situation. Unfortunately, there *are* poorly handled trades on the part of professionally managed institutions and an institution's trading ability may not live up to its research skills.

Sales May Set a Trend. Just as other institutions, brokerage firms, and individual investors sometimes use institutional buying as a guide for their own investments, those firms and individuals may use institutional selling as a signal to unload their holdings as well.

Mutual Fund Redemptions Can Force Stock Sales. While institutions generally sell stock on the basis of an investment decision, this may not necessarily be so with mutual funds. Their own holders can indirectly affect selling decisions, because mutual funds stand ready to redeem their shares on demand. If there is an unusually high redemption demand, the mutual fund will have to liquidate some holdings to raise cash. As a result, good, solid holdings which would not normally be sold may have to be put on the market.

Interference with Management's Decisions. An institution that approves of most of a company's activities may disagree with a specific proposal. A proposed acquisition or merger occasionally may raise objections on the institution's part. Generally, however, there is no question that most institutions would rather not be involved in a situation where they disagree with the management of one of the companies whose stock they hold in their portfolio. As a rule, when a fund is disenchanted with a company, it sells; it does not attempt to reshape the company.

Demands for Extra Detailed Financial Data. The size of an institution's holdings, the comparative difficulty it has in selling stock because of the large numbers of shares involved, and its more professional approach to investing may lead it to demand information from a company not normally given to other security analysts. These requests on the part of institutional analysts may seek monthly sales and earnings statements, profits and sales by divisions, profits or profit margins by product, and test-market results. Despite the institution's obvious need for as much financial information as possible, *a company should never give information to an analyst from an institution that the company is not prepared to give to an analyst from a brokerage house.* To give more to an institution and less to other analysts is to treat the institution as an insider.

No institution is privileged to have extra information that might allow it to buy or sell a stock when other investors might be doing the opposite because they do not have the same information.

STIMULATING INVESTMENT INTEREST

A company—unless it be one of the "institutional favorites" —cannot sit back and wait for institutional investors to knock on management's door. On the contrary, it is necessary for management to seek out those institutions that realistically might be stockholder candidates. The word "realistically" is used because not all institutions are potential candidates.

For example: Some institutions have minimum size requirements concerning the number of shares available for public trading; other institutions prefer income stocks; still other institutions prefer to invest in growth stocks; some look for special situations; and there are others who favor a select group of industries and refuse to consider companies outside those boundaries. Nevertheless, there are scores and scores of suitable institutions for almost every publicly owned company. The trick is to seek them out.

Finding the Right Institutions. To determine which institutions might be potential purchasers of a company's stock, an analysis must be made of the various institutions:

PUBLICLY OWNED INSTITUTIONS. The investment companies that publish their portfolios—the mutual funds and the closed-end investment companies—make it relatively easy to determine their interest and requirements. Management can read their portfolios to ascertain the types of investments that the institutions favor. When likely institutional stockholder candidates are discovered, management should add their names to a list of institutions that are potential investors in their company's stock.

HIDDEN INSTITUTIONS. Unfortunately, the institutions that do not publish their portfolios are by far in the majority. It is obviously more difficult to determine which of these institutions are prospective stockholders. To get an insight into what hundreds of non-publicly owned institutions are seeking demands that management maintain a close relationship with the financial community. There is always a good deal of knowledge circulating on what specific institutions are or are not interested in buying at any given time. A company with good sources of Wall Street information can ferret out potential institutional investors.

INSTITUTIONAL BROKERAGE FIRMS.   There is a special breed of stock broker: the institutional brokerage house. Such firms have close relationships with many institutions, know their requirements, and direct their custom-made, in-depth research reports exclusively toward them. As a result of such catering to the "wholesale" buyer of securities, institutions today rely on those brokers for many of their investment ideas. Consequently, these institutional brokerage houses have it in their power to bring a new company to the attention of institutional buyers. Realistically, however, institutional brokerage houses find it more profitable to do research studies for their institutional clients on the larger corporations listed on the New York Stock Exchange because more shares are available to sell to the bigger institutions. Nevertheless, small, well-run, little-known companies do get a hearing at times from institutional brokerage houses and are sometimes recommended to institutional investors.

Among the brokerage firms in New York City that concentrate on institution-oriented research are: Auerbach, Pollak & Richardson, Inc.; Burnham & Co.; Dominick & Dominick, Inc.; Donaldson, Lufkin & Jenrette, Inc.; Drexel, Harriman & Ripley, Inc.; Faulkner, Dawkins & Sullivan; Goldman, Sachs & Co.; Jesup & Lamont; Laird & Company, Corp.; H. C. Wainwright & Co.; and White, Weld & Co. For many companies, working with these specialized brokerage firms can be as important as working with institutional investors on a personal, direct basis.

Developing Direct Relationship with Institution.   Once management has compiled a list of institutions that appear to be logical candidates for stockholders, it is necessary to foster their interest in the company. There are several ways—all of which should be employed—for management to bring itself to the attention of those institutional investors. Many of these methods have already been pointed out in previous chapters dealing with security analysts; the emphasis here is on *institutional* analysts.

MAILINGS.   Obviously, an analyst employed in the research department of an institution cannot evaluate a company unless he knows something about it. Thus, management must give the analyst information about the company's financial progress and strength from a statistical viewpoint. The specific analyst who follows the company's industry should be sent the company's Financial Fact Book, copies of its most recent annual reports, interim reports, and other information that will help him understand the company. This analyst's name must also be added to the regular analyst mailing list so that he will receive all pertinent news about the company. (For a list of items that should be mailed to security analysts, see Chapter 11, page 146.)

INFORMAL MEETINGS.   The interchange of ideas with management that takes place in a brief two hours over lunch can develop interest in a company on the part of institutional analysts. These informal meetings—which should not include more than eight or ten analysts at a time—are most effective when they are restricted to analysts only from institutions or brokerage firms that deal with institutions.

While the informal luncheon usually is arranged by the company, there are times when a brokerage firm—often the company's investment banker—will arrange an informal meeting for institutional analysts to meet with company executives.

PERSONAL INTERVIEWS WITH INSTITUTIONAL ANALYSTS. While such an approach is time-consuming, the personal interview can do a great deal to acquaint the institutional analyst with management, the company's policies, and its future plans.

Helping Institutions To Buy and Sell.   Because institutions take substantial positions in the stock they purchase, they prefer to buy and sell in large blocks. By doing so, they know exactly where they stand with a particular security and do not have to worry about price fluctuations that might stop them from completing the transaction. Many institutions will not purchase a relatively inactive stock unless a block is available. Some institutions will buy an initial block—even though it does not meet their total requirements—and buy additional stock on the open market. This means that a company may be able to attract an institution if it can assist it in obtaining even a small block of stock.

A company should always be ready, when possible, to assist major stockholders, institutions, and individuals who wish to buy or sell a large block of stock. Armed with such knowledge, the company may be able to put a large potential seller in touch with an institution that is interested in buying a large block. Conversely, if an institution is interested in eliminating or reducing its position, another institution that has shown an interest in the company may be willing to buy the block or an institution which has already taken a position in the stock may want to increase its holdings. A company that can bring both parties together not only will be performing a service for both of them, but will keep the stock from being buffeted by a large transaction on the open market. Litton Industries, Inc., for example, has one individual in the company who is designated to receive calls about blocks for sale or purchase. This person tries to get large buyers and sellers together so that they can work things out themselves.

If a company learns from a brokerage firm that an institution wishes to buy or sell the company's stock, the company must scrupulously see that any help it gives the institution to buy or sell its stock is done through that brokerage firm. In addition, the company should not let others learn about this transaction before it becomes publicly known.

III

STOCKHOLDERS AND THE FINANCIAL PRESS

13

Broadening Stock Ownership

One of the prime objectives in any investor relations program is to increase the number of a company's stockholders. Without a broad stockholder base, no other aspect of the investor relations program will function to its fullest potential. For example, if the company has few stockholders, its securities will sell in a thin, volatile market, brokerage firms will hesitate to recommend its stock, and institutional investors will tend to ignore the company.

Although all companies stand to benefit from an expansion of their stockholder lists, a company whose stock is not widely distributed has the most to gain. The smaller a company's stockholder base, the more important it becomes to expand it.

How big, then, must that stockholder base be? For practical purposes, the answer is: A company cannot have too many stockholders—there is no limit. The number of stockholders a company has will be primarily influenced by the number of shares in public hands, the length of time the company has been public, and the effectiveness of a company's efforts to broaden its stockholder base.

The goal of a broad stockholder base cannot be achieved overnight. Stockholders must be acquired deliberately on a long-range, year-in-year-out basis. American Telephone and Telegraph Company with a stockholder list in the three million category is still actively striving to broaden the base of its stock ownership. As far back as 1927, Walter S. Gifford, the then president of A.T.&T., was publicly discussing the importance to his company of developing a large and satisfied stockholder group. Still seeking to expand the number of its stockholders today, A.T.&T. has attained a large stockholder base which can be frequently tapped for new capital and can be expected to stand behind the company in any government regulatory controversy.

Since there is no such thing as too many stockholders—and since gaining more and more stockholders is a long-term proposition—management cannot afford to relegate this investor-relations project to the end of a long list of things to be accomplished some day in the future. On the contrary, broadening the stockholder base must be a continuous program that management actively fosters.

REASONS FOR BROADENING STOCK OWNERSHIP

Better, More Attractive Market for Stock. Trading activity in a particular security is closely related to the number of stockholders owning shares in the company. The more stockholders there are, the greater the trading activity that can be expected. Therefore, a substantial increase in the number of shareholders will almost always produce a substantial increase in that stock's trading volume.

High trading volume is important because it helps maintain a relatively stable price in the stock on a day-to-day basis. It is almost axiomatic on Wall Street that the less trading in a stock, the greater will be the spread between the bid and asked price. Such "gaps" almost universally bring about wide price fluctuations from one transaction to the next. Obviously, stocks that fluctuate widely in price on limited volume have investment drawbacks.

High trading volume has other major—and closely related —benefits: It enables holders of large blocks of stock to sell easily without upsetting the price severely. As an example, it is apparent that it is far easier for an investor to sell 1,000 shares of a stock that trades an average of 5,000 shares a day than it would be if that same investor wanted to sell 1,000 shares when only an average of 500 shares traded each day.

Before an institution will consider investing in a company's stock, that institution will examine the stock's trading activity to determine the ease with which it will be able to buy and sell. As a natural consequence, the higher the trading activity, the greater the number of institutional investors that will become interested and the larger will be the size of those institutions.

The broader the stockholder base—with consequent superior marketability of stock—the better the chance for a company to make an acquisition. One of the reasons an owner of a small business frequently will want to be acquired is to obtain a security that can be readily sold rather than have his personal portfolio locked into a company whose stock is not marketable. A company not widely owned would not be able to satisfy such a person's requirements for a stock that can easily be sold.

Ease of Raising Money.   The more stockholders on the company's roster, the larger is that company's potential source of capital in a rights offering. This has proved especially important for companies—such as utilities—that must sell stock every few years. On the other hand, a company with an already relatively broad-based stockholder list will find it easy to sell a new stock offering to the general public because broad-based companies have great appeal to investors.

Customers for Company Products.   Since stockholders in a company have a built-in bias toward that company, they tend —on balance—to buy their company's products. Companies that have conducted research along such lines have discovered that there is *significantly* greater usage of their products among stockholders than among non-stockholders. Moreover, stock-holders become product boosters, frequently "selling" the merits of an item to friends. Certainly, in terms of *total* sales, the added volume generated from a company's stockholders is small for most companies. Yet, these added sales are a plus factor not to be overlooked.

Voter Support for Legislative Goals.   Utilities frequently seek rate increases and are very much aware that stockholders are more likely to recognize the necessity for such increases in the rate structure than non-stockholders. Today, the growth of governmental influence on business in general has stretched far beyond the point where only quasi-public corporations are affected. Pressures from the government on individual com-panies and on specific industries, such as drug companies or auto manufacturers, have made it important for corporations as a whole to have vast "armies" of stockholders who will side with management in its free-enterprise endeavors.

TECHNIQUES FOR BROADENING STOCKHOLDER BASE

Offering Additional Stock.   The sale of common stock—whether a new issue or a secondary offering—automatically opens up opportunities for acquiring new stockholders by increasing the number of shares in public hands.

Thin markets are often caused by an insufficient floating supply of stock. For example: A company may have 1 million shares outstanding, with 600,000 shares in the hands of man-agement and a few large stockholders. In such a case, if the company itself does not need to raise additional capital, major stockholders should be looked to to increase the floating supply of stock through a secondary offering. When a bright future for the company seems assured, it is often difficult to persuade large stockholders that their own interests might be better served by selling a portion of their holdings. If these stock-holders refuse to sell, keeping the floating supply below an adequate level, the company's stock—including their own holdings, of course—may well suffer no matter how bright the outlook for the company appears. While the sale of potentially profitable shares of stock on the part of large holders may *appear* costly in the light of anticipated events, it might well be the most profitable course of action in the long-run provided the investment appeal of the remaining securities is improved.

Stock Splits. Splits lower the stock's price. And lower prices tend to attract more stockholders. More important, stock splits increase the *total* number of shares available for purchase (for details see Chapter 2).

Acquisition of Companies. Perhaps the quickest way to broaden the stockholder base is to acquire another publicly owned company through an exchange of stock. This automatically brings to the acquiring company all the stockholders of the acquired company. Although no company would make an acquisition solely to add more stockholders to its roster, the benefits of a broader stockholder base ought to be weighed when considering an acquisition.

Forcing Conversion. When a company has an outstanding convertible debenture or preferred stock, chances are that those securities are held by many investors who are *not* common stockholders of the company. Forcing conversion (see Chapter 3) of such securities will automatically turn many of those investors into common stockholders.

Expanding Geographic Spread of Stock Ownership. As additional shares are added to the floating supply, management should attempt to spread stock ownership around the country. This will provide a wide base for raising future capital and make it easier to gain the support of the investment community in areas other than only one or two major financial centers or the company's local operating area. There are several avenues management may follow to attract stockholders from areas where there is little or no stockholder concentration. Among them are:

1. Hold small meetings with security analysts from local brokerage firms and commercial banks.

2. Address local security analyst society meetings.

3. If there is a company plant in a region of low stockholder ownership, arrange plant tours for local business and social groups.

4. Arrange interviews between the company president and financial editors of newspapers serving areas of low stock ownership.

5. Make certain the stock's price is quoted in local newspapers. It is difficult to interest potential stockholders if they are unable to find a company's stock quotation. Many large newspapers throughout the nation do not list the closing prices of all New York Stock Exchange firms and over-the-counter companies.

A survey of the daily newspapers throughout the country will determine which newspapers are publishing quotations and which are not. Whenever an appreciable number of stockholders exists in an area served by a non-quoting newspaper, a letter should be sent to the newspaper's financial editor. This letter should point out the number of local stockholders in the newspaper's circulation area who are unable to find the price of the stock they own. Frequently, the financial editor will see to it that the omission is corrected.

A company whose stock is traded in the over-the-counter market may have to add a preliminary step to the procedure and obtain approval from the National Association of Security Dealers before it can increase the number of newspapers publishing its stock quotation.

INADVISABILITY OF BUYING OUT SMALL STOCKHOLDERS

Although it is apparent that companies should actively try to broaden their base of stock ownership, some have taken actions that have accomplished the exact opposite. These companies—believing they were burdened with the cost of serving too many small stockholders—have tried to eliminate their odd-lot holders by offering to buy their stock. A company faced with many small stockholders is better advised to attempt to make them bigger stockholders through an effective stock-holder relations program, as well as through subsequent stock splits as the company grows.

There are certain unusual situations that bring about a disproportionate number of small stockholders that have caused companies to consider buying them out. Among these situations are:

1. A merger in which round-lot stockholders of the acquired company receive only a few shares of the acquiring company
2. A reverse split so that the number of shares held by each stockholder is substantially reduced (It was a 1-for-4 reverse split that prompted Monogram Industries, Inc., to offer to redeem the common stock of shareholders owning 40 or fewer shares.)
3. A reorganization that gives stockholders fewer shares than they held before
4. A distribution by a company to its stockholders of stock it holds in another corporation (Such was the situation that faced Canal-Randolph Corp. which offered to acquire all the holdings of its stockholders who owned 24 or fewer shares. The company estimated that lots of 24 shares or less were held by 4,400 of its 11,000 shareholders and that it cost the company from $3.50 to $4 a year per shareholder. Most of the small blocks were held by former stockholders of Kratter Corp. which distributed to its shareholders most of its holdings in Canal-Randolph.)

Results of offers to buy out small stockholders have varied considerably from company to company. Ling-Temco-Vought, Inc., considered its offer to be moderately successful when approximately 35 per cent of the holders of 10 shares or less tendered their stock for purchase by the company.

Curtiss-Wright Corporation received a tender of 38,000 shares from 3,500 stockholders who owned 25 shares or less. The United Corporation eliminated 1,184 stockholders by buying back first 5,044 shares from stockholders holding 9 shares or less and 2,700 additional stockholders when the company widened its offer to include holders of 20 shares or less. Victoreen Instrument Company eliminated 450 out of 4,000 small stockholders with its first offer and an additional 300 when it repeated the offer a year later.

Offers to buy out small stockholders have been infrequent. Consequently, there is not sufficient statistical evidence to indicate what percentage of stockholders could be expected to tender their stock. The experience of Ling-Temco-Vought in eliminating 35 per cent of its small stockholders may be as much as can be expected by any company. Most companies will find it difficult to match that result.

14

Stockholder
Communications

Communication is the backbone of any stockholder relations program. It is one of the most important factors in cementing shareowner goodwill and loyalty. Most publicly owned companies communicate with their stockholders at least 11 times a year: three quarterly reports, a preliminary earnings report, an annual report (see Chapter 15 for a discussion of the annual report), four dividend checks, a post-annual-meeting report, and a proxy statement. Apart from such routine communications, management frequently writes to stockholders on many other *special* occasions, sending such items as: letters of welcome to new stockholders; news announcements concerning mergers, acquisitions, stock splits, labor difficulties, etc.; reprints of speeches; and mailings of company products.

How frequently a company communicates with its stockholders is only one factor affecting good stockholder relations. *What* management says is obviously even more important.

Unfortunately, many companies do not place sufficient emphasis on the all-important "what" aspects of their program. On the contrary, it appears that fulfilling the obligation to send messages to stockholders at periodic intervals is often the main consideration. Many stockholders react unfavorably towards letters that are filled with platitudes and avoid problems or discussions of anticipated results.

Since stockholders are not united, as a group they bring little or no pressure to bear on management for more complete information, although major stockholders—such as institutional investors—do make their weight felt individually. Yet, it must be remembered that all stockholders—not just the major ones—are quite literally partners in the company's business and deserve to be told in concrete terms what is happening to their company. And they can best be informed by a company president who adopts the attitude that he will let them in on his thinking by explaining in his stockholder communications the type of things—although in simpler terms and probably in less detail—that he would readily tell a security analyst in a personal interview.

ROUTINE COMMUNICATIONS

Preliminary Earnings Announcements. A brief preliminary report should be sent to stockholders as soon as audited annual figures are available—usually three to five weeks before the formal annual report can be printed and mailed. Such a preliminary report need not be an elaborate one, but it should include significant comparative figures along with a brief mention of the year's highlights.

Quarterly Reports. Sales and earnings figures should be reported on a quarterly basis simultaneously to the press and the stockholders. These reports should be issued as soon as feasible but never more than 30 days after the close of the quarter.

The interim figures reported to stockholders should include the cumulative total for the current fiscal year—such as six-month or nine-month figures—as well as figures for the latest quarter. The rare companies that experience seasonal variations so great that three-month figures might confuse stock-holders can include cumulative latest 12-month figures in addition to the latest three-month figures.

Quarterly statements should do more than report on sales and earnings for the most recent quarter. For one thing, such reports should always include comparative figures for the similar period of the previous year, usually spelling out percentage changes. And the report should go beyond the mere statistical setting down of figures. Some light should be shed on the company's activities in the quarter, with description in some detail of the factors that improved or adversely affected that period's sales and earnings. Such observations should be candid, especially when sales, earnings, or profit margins are down.

In addition to reviewing the results of the past quarter, management should also tell stockholders what the outlook is for the company during the next quarter and for the remainder of the year. Actual sales and earnings projections are not necessary, but some indication of the company's expectations should be given.

Dividends. Any *special* news concerning a dividend—an increase, an extra, a cutback—should be mailed immediately to the stockholder. It is not necessary to mail announcements of regular dividend declarations that are unchanged from previous quarters.

It is also helpful to summarize for stockholders early each year the company's dividend record during the previous year, including the record dates, payment dates, and per-share payments for *each* dividend so the shareowner can not only compute his income taxes accurately but also verify that he received all his dividend payments. If a company's dividend is either not fully taxable or is only partially taxable on a capital-gains basis, stockholders should be told so as soon as possible following the year end.

Dividend checks should be mailed separately from quarterly

reports. When check and report are enclosed in the same envelope, the stockholder pays less attention to the quarterly report.

While dividend checks alone have built-in stockholder goodwill properties, enclosures may also be sent *when appropriate*. Typical dividend enclosures include: new product literature; news announcements specifically about the dividend, such as a change in the rate; and details of an impending stock dividend or a stock split, even though the news has already been mailed to stockholders at the time the announcement was initially made.

There is some information that should be imprinted on the check itself—for example, dividend payments per share, record dates, and change of address requests.

Proxy Statements.   Proxy statements—usually necessary only once a year—are generally dull but legally necessary documents. To make the proxy statement more readable some companies such as Mobil Oil Company, Inc., American Electric Power Company, Inc., and Ford Motor Company, have included a photograph and a short biographical sketch of each director up for election. United States Steel Corporation has used the proxy statement to discuss the function of its board of directors and how it operates.

There may be occasions other than the annual meeting when a company may have to seek stockholder approval and issue a proxy statement. These may involve an acquisition or merger, a change of the company's name, a stock split, authorization of additional shares, or a change in the corporation's structure.

Report of Annual Meeting.   No matter how successful a company is in attracting a large attendance to its annual meeting, the vast majority of its stockholders will not be present. The post-annual-meeting report gives management an opportunity to tell absent stockholders what occurred.

Among companies that understand the importance of a post-meeting report and publish one for their stockholders there is substantial variance in opinion as to what should and should not be included. Some large corporations send out verbatim transcripts of the entire meeting—word for word, the good with the bad. Other companies—typically, but not exclusively, the smaller companies—publish only the barest summary of the meeting. For example, in one post-meeting report Xerox Corporation included everything except the cat-calls, hisses, and boos. That same year Otis Elevator Company summarized its annual meeting in two pages and described the question period as follows: "At the conclusion of his remarks the President answered a number of questions asked by the stockholders present." No indication was given of what the questions and answers were.

The trend is for companies to publish post-annual meeting reports that include fairly complete presentations of both the speeches and the question period.

Much of the difficulty that surrounds the publication of a post-meeting report hinges on the editing. Editing is necessary because a verbatim transcript of an annual meeting contains dull pages of repetitions and trivia. Once a company under-takes to eliminate dull passages, however, it places itself in the role of a censor. Management must make sure that this role is not abused. It must never delete or modify questions and comments that are embarrassing. The stockholder has a right to know about them.

SPECIAL COMMUNICATIONS

In addition to the routine mailings, there are many other worthwhile opportunities to communicate with stockholders. Many companies do not take sufficient advantage of these opportunities and mail only a terse annual report. Other com-panies go to the opposite extreme and flood their stockholders with as many as thirty communications in one year. The cor-rect balance must be found for each company. Each mailing should meet the test of pertinence or timeliness.

Special Announcements. Whenever a newsworthy event takes place, not only the press but the stockholders as well ought to be informed immediately. In fact, the mailings to stockholders should be timed to coincide with releases to the press so that the majority of stockholders will receive the news in their mail on the same morning that the story is reported in the daily newspapers.

It is frequently difficult to determine whether or not a particular event is significant enough to be reported to stockholders immediately. For example, most acquisitions are important and ought to be announced to stockholders at the same time as to the press. Yet, it is possible for a relatively large company to acquire a company small enough to make no appreciable change in the immediate earnings outlook. In such instances, the management of the acquiring company may wait until the next quarterly report to inform stockholders of the acquisition.

As another example, a strike affecting one factory of a multi-plant company is usually not significant, but a strike that affects an important part of a company's operations can be. When a major labor problem erupts, stockholders should be informed immediately about the extent of the strike, the issues involved, and why management is taking the stand it is. Similarly, when a major strike is finally settled, stockholders should be told how the work stoppage affected sales and earnings, and how the new settlement will affect future earnings.

Perhaps the simplest way to determine whether or not to inform stockholders immediately is to answer this question: Will the event to be reported substantially affect either earnings or the nature of the business? If the answer is "Yes," stockholders should be informed immediately.

Typical of the news events warranting special announcements to stockholders are these:

1. Development of a *major* new product
2. An important mineral discovery
3. An acquisition or a merger
4. A rumor that should be contradicted or confirmed
5. Major strikes
6. Listing on a stock exchange

Reprints.   Reprinting and mailing a speech or a magazine article is an excellent way to keep the shareowners informed about company developments. At the same time, reprints should be used sparingly. A stockholder barraged with a dozen —or even a half dozen—reprints a year from one company will soon be throwing envelopes into the waste basket without bothering to open them.

Mailing a reprint of an executive's speech before a major security analysts' society is a legitimate use of this communications tool. However, a reprint of a speech about general topics before a civic group—to cite one example—will cause stockholders to wonder why the company spends so much money on promotional literature. In choosing the type of material to be reprinted, the best rule is this: If the information *significantly* furthers the stockholders' insight into the company or its industry, then it is worth reprinting. There is just one exception to that rule: A company should *never* send stockholders a reprint of a brokerage firm's recommendation of its stock. Such a reprint is not only in bad taste but gives stockholders the impression that management is recommending that they buy more of the company's stock.

Company Magazines.   A company magazine that is not designed specifically for the stockholder is, at best, of marginal interest to him. This is especially true when it is a product of the personnel department oriented primarily towards the employee and local company events.

Some company magazines do aim a number of their articles in the general direction of the stockholder. *The Inch,* published by the Texas Eastern Transmission Corporation, is one such publication. Its pages are filled with lively discussions of topics relating to the company's business. One article explained leverage financing, an important aspect of Texas Eastern's business, in simple terms for the stockholder.

Any management that undertakes a regular publication to be sent to stockholders must be prepared to turn out a superlative one. Anything short of that goal will defeat its purpose. Some companies recognize that many stockholders will not want to receive the company magazine and send it only to those who have indicated they would like to read it.

Letters of Welcome.   The first communication management sends a new stockholder is a critical document because it sets the tone for their relationship. If the stockholder's first experience with a company is a good one, he will tend to continue to judge company activities in a favorable light.

One way to enhance management's chances of starting off its relationship with a new stockholder on a sound footing is to mail him a letter of welcome. Such a letter lets the stockholder know the company recognizes that he has become a part owner of the enterprise and that his investment is appreciated. A letter of welcome should appear to be an individually typed, individually signed letter.

A well-composed letter of welcome should contain these features:

1. A description of the company's business activities and background
2. An explanation of the company's philosophy and direction
3. A statement on the company's dividend policy and, if possible, a schedule of the approximate dates when the stockholder can expect to receive dividend checks
4. A promise that he will hear from the company regularly
5. An invitation to write management about any question he may have

Enclosed with the letter of welcome should be the company's latest annual report, its latest interim statement, and, if available, a brochure that describes the company. As an added impression builder, samples of corporate products can be sent (see below, page 183). Scott Paper Company, for example, sends a large assortment of its paper products to each new stockholder.

The opposite of the letter of welcome is the letter of regret that some companies send to stockholders when they sell their stock. This type of letter can be easily misconstrued by the stockholder and is not recommended. No matter how well written, the letter of regret tends to put the recipient on the defensive. Despite the fact that some stockholders react well to such a letter, the negative reaction of others makes the over-all value highly questionable.

Letters of Recognition. These letters are relatively new to the corporate scene. They provide management with a means of cementing relations with stockholders of long standing. Based on the premise that everyone likes to be treated as some-one special, letters of recognition are sent to stockholders on their anniversaries as investors in the company, such as the 10th, 20th, or 25th year as a stockholder of record. Such a letter should be typewritten on the president's stationery and individually signed. The more personal the letter is made to appear the more effective it will be. A letter of recognition says, in effect, "Today marks the 20th anniversary of your having become a stockholder in our company. We want you to know that we appreciate this long relationship and look forward to many more years of our association."

Product Samples. Companies that send samples of their products to stockholders find an enthusiastic response to such mailings. Almost all people like to get something for nothing, and stockholders are no exception. A mailing of corporate products is indicated primarily when a company makes a relatively inexpensive, easily shipped consumer product.

Stockholders' appreciation of the gift goes far beyond the intrinsic value of the product. For example, one company that sent some of its products to its stockholders just before Christmas was deluged with "thank-you" letters from some 50% of the happy recipients. This is also a good way to acquaint the stockholder with a new product that is expected to generate large sales.

Stockholder Correspondence. A stockholder who writes to his company deserves a prompt and thoughtful reply. Even the short notes some stockholders scribble on the back of a proxy card should be answered, although an answer may not actually be called for. However, for the most part, stockholders rarely write, and most companies with medium-sized stock-holder lists will get no more than one or two letters a week from their stockholders.

Letters from stockholders addressed to the president of the company are best answered by him—even when someone else does the drafting of the letter. If the stockholder, however, is seeking some specialized information, then the president may refer the letter to another corporate executive who is more familiar with the subject. Correspondence concerning stock transfers, lost dividend checks, change of address, or other matters relating to stockholder records may be handled by the corporate secretary.

A company that has hundreds of thousands of stockholders may receive many letters a week. When the volume grows so that it becomes literally impossible for any one executive to answer all the stockholder mail addressed to him, other executives must be given the responsibility of responding. It is, in any event, best to have stockholder correspondence signed by a company officer. Stockholders want to feel they are getting attention from a high executive, not a minor functionary.

Promptness in answering a stockholder is a necessity. Except in unusual circumstances, a reply should be on the way within twenty-four hours after receipt of his letter.

Letters from stockholders whose tone indicates that they are less than happy with the way the company is being run should be handled with care and patience. This is a good opportunity to turn a disgruntled stockholder into a friendly one.

Other Communications.   There are many other good opportunities to communicate with stockholders and companies should take advantage of them. In connection with the 1964–65 New York World's Fair, several companies that had large exhibits sent tickets to stockholders so they would not have to wait on line.

Films of interest to the general public can be offered to stockholders. Parke, Davis & Company produced a motion picture in sound and color entitled "Counter–Attack!" which tells the story of the American drug industry in assisting other countries to solve their health problems. The company offered the half-hour film to its stockholders, without charge, for showing to any interested group.

A brochure that describes a company's operations should be mailed to stockholders—even though not designed for that purpose—if it gives a good non-technical description of the company.

Important anniversaries are often occasions to prepare special publications for stockholders. Drexel Enterprises, Inc., sent each of its stockholders a ninety-two page book on "Sixty Years of Progress in the Making of Fine Furniture." The Warner Brothers Company, on its 90th anniversary, sent each of its stockholders a special hard-cover, 112-page book which traced the growth of the company since its founding.

Special corporate events can be the occasion of sending stockholders a letter of invitation. For example, they can be invited to attend the opening of a new plant or store, if they live in reasonable proximity to the new facility.

15

The Annual Report

No longer is the annual report a statistical record suitable only for the stockholder with an accountant's mind. On the contrary, today's annual report has become a most important medium for management in communicating with its stockholders, potential stockholders, and security analysts. Since every annual report, whether good or bad, gives the stockholder an impression of the company, it is certainly to management's advantage to make the impression that is given a desired one.

Whether or not any one annual report reaches its potential for communicating depends more on the thinking that goes into it than on the money spent on it. The more of an annual report a company can get its stockholders to read, the greater the opportunity to present its message. This is a worthwhile goal because a well-informed stockholder is a loyal stockholder; a well-informed security analyst—one who finds in an annual report the many detailed items he needs to appraise a company—will be more likely to recommend that company.

Almost every annual report can be improved. Management must learn to highlight the items that are of interest to stockholders—not the items of interest to management. Only in this way can an annual report be an effective vehicle for communicating to the stockholder and giving him a clear understanding of what the company is doing, what it intends to do, what its strong points are, its problems, and the economics of its industry.

STUDY OF THE REPORT'S AUDIENCE

The first step toward improving an annual report's ability to communicate is a critical examination of the audience: "*Who* is going to read the report?" and "*What* does the audience want from this publication?"

When both of those questions have been answered, management will see that it has a clear picture of the communications problems its report must overcome.

Who is the Audience?   The audience for the typical annual report is actually *two* quite separate audiences. The *stockholder* is the primary audience. On average, he will read only a fragment of the report. It is not that he is unreceptive. On the contrary, more often than not he feels he has an obligation to read the annual report of a company in which he has invested his money. However, much of an annual report is usually too technical—and sometimes too dull—to keep him interested. Capturing the stockholder's attention demands the best use of the journalistic arts: simplicity of presentation, readability, and strong picture content are the qualities to be sought.

The *security analyst* is the secondary audience. He should read the entire report because his livelihood depends on his knowledge. However, each annual report must compete with many others for a security analyst's attention—particularly since so many are issued at approximately the same time. Realistically, not every security analyst reads every report in its entirety that he should. A well-organized report will help get his attention. A complete report will provide him with the information he needs.

What Interests the Stockholder?   The *stockholder* wants to know how his company is doing. Is money being made? Will more money be made in the future? Readership studies point out that the stockholder most often reads the financial highlights, the president's letter, and the feature sections that describe the company's business.

Ideally, to keep the stockholder's interest, the financial highlights should be on the first left-hand page and the president's letter on the facing right-hand page. A readership study by one major company indicated that a photograph of the president on the same page as the president's letter will substantially increase readership of that page—possibly as much as 40 per cent.

What Does Not Interest the Stockholder?   Unfortunately, random surveys of annual reports show that many companies continue to publish dull lists of officers and directors, or of regional offices, in the prime-viewing portion—the opening pages—of the report. Such lists are not sufficiently interesting to the reader to warrant up-front treatment.

The stockholder has little interest in a large photo of fifteen directors grouped together in a crowded board room. Nor does he get excited by an architect's rendering of a new plant or a new factory or a new headquarters building or photographs of the company's production machinery. Furthermore, the stockholder cares little about the company's organizational chart with its names and titles in small print all interconnected with red and blue and black lines or with lists of plants and sales offices. He also has only passing interest in stockholder analysis breakdowns, employee relations, and compensation arrangements.

This is not to say that many of the items with little stockholder interest mentioned above—from lists of directors and officers through stockholder analyses—should not appear in the report. They can, naturally, but they ought to be kept in proper proportion. They are necessary as reference items.

They should not be mistaken for interesting feature material. Therefore, in order not to impair readership, they should be relegated to a position at the back of the report.

What Interests the Security Analyst? By contrast with the stockholder, the security analyst seeks facts and statistics— especially those that go beyond the routine. For example, the analyst has come to accept as routine a company's recapitulation of the past year's accomplishments, its pointing with pride toward new products and their ultimate effect on the market, and its optimistic outlook for the years ahead. What he wants are breakdowns that in most instances only the company can supply. He also likes to find statistical ratios presented in the annual report. Otherwise, laborious calculations are required on his part to obtain this information. The most important facts and statistics the security analyst seeks are these:

DIVISIONAL SALES BREAKDOWNS. Without such information, an analyst is forced to guess where the bulk of a company's business lies. Many times an analyst prefers not to guess and, instead, will refuse to recommend the stock of a company that may or may not be outstanding in its sports equipment sales when school furniture and books are the other divisions of the company. Consequently, a divisional sales breakdown is a necessary item for any diversified company.

DIVISIONAL EARNINGS BREAKDOWNS. The analyst needs this information for the same reason he needs the sales breakdowns: to evaluate accurately the company's accomplishments. Although most companies still refuse to provide earnings breakdowns, such a demand on the analyst's part is not unreasonable. For example, while an analyst may know that 60% of a company's sales are in sports equipment, 30% in school furniture, and 10% in books, he may still be misled unless he knows that 53% of net income comes from the sale of school furniture.

Profit breakdowns may sometimes have to be withheld if

they provide information that can help competition. Usually, however, divisions have such diverse product mixes that profit breakdowns will hide margins of individual products.

If a company believes it must not reveal profit breakdowns, it should at least provide the relative profitability of each division. Thus, to follow through with the above example, the company would report that school furniture contributed most to earnings, followed by sports equipment and books. And it might also say that school furniture carried the highest profit margin, followed by books and sports equipment.

TEN-YEAR FINANCIAL SUMMARY. An analyst likes such statistical "histories" because they save him from having to make his own, using the company's previous nine reports as his source material. Such reviews of the past decade are so commonplace today—for companies that have audited figures for that many years, naturally—that any review that covers less than those "magic" ten years may become suspect. Analysts may assume that management is hiding something unfavorable.

In addition to items from the income and balance sheet statements, ratios such as profit margins, return on capital, tax rates, dividend payout, current ratio, debt-equity ratio, growth rates, and other pertinent calculations should be presented in this review.

One item included in the 10-year reviews of some companies that stockholders find interesting is the price range of the company's stock in each of those ten years. Another item of growing importance is the trading volume—a tabulation of weekly or monthly or annual volume. Since institutional investors make stock commitments in sizeable quantities, such trading volume figures make it simpler for the institution to determine the ease with which it can buy and sell the stock.

PLANNING THE REPORT

An effective annual report—one that gives the reader an understanding of the company—must be more than a document that meets the factual needs of its stockholder and security analyst audiences. It must also be attractive and attention getting, or it will fail in its purpose.

The annual report must highlight what most interests the stockholder, must play down what the stockholder finds of least interest, must have the ring of honesty, must invite reading with eye-catching photographs and an appealing layout, and—finally—must project the company's desired image from cover to cover. The annual report must be designed for the busy reader—the one who just skims through the report— and tell this reader a good deal of the company story in just headlines, pictures, charts, and captions.

Perhaps the easiest way to understand just what is required is to study successful consumer-oriented magazines. These magazines make excellent "textbooks." For example, in addition to their normal readership from subscribers and regular newsstand purchasers, they "fight" for bonus circulation through additional newsstand sales by trying to grab the passer-by's attention with their cover. An annual report cover should have similar attention-getting characteristics.

An appealing layout invites stockholder readership. *Life* magazine serves as an outstanding example of how elements on a page—text, headlines, photos, and captions—can be arranged so they pull the reader into the magazine, getting him to read page after page. The pictures *Life* uses are dramatic, have been taken as close to the subject as possible to eliminate unimportant details, are well lighted, and—most importantly —are inherently interesting.

Whenever in doubt as to the effectiveness of any particular layout, simplicity of design should rule. A cluttered page repels the reader.

A company must judge each element that goes into the annual report—text, headlines, photos, captions, charts, illustrations, and graphs—in the light of the specific image it seeks to portray.

For example, a company in New England that spent quite heavily on research—more than its competitors—was never known as a research-minded company to the financial community. Recognizing this, the company launched a long-term concerted effort to overcome such an attitude. Its annual report covers showed four-color dramatic photos of scientists working in the research laboratory; each president's letter pointed to the year's research accomplishments; the text of each annual report featured a different slice of the research department's functions; the company reversed its policy on not revealing research expenditures so that graphs illustrating such outlays could be published in the annual report, and the sales volume from products developed in the company's laboratories was disclosed so that the investment community would realize the effect of the company's research accomplishments.

The Cover.   The annual report cover should do two things. It should give stockholders an overall impression of the company, and it should make them want to find out what is inside the report. This can be accomplished by the following techniques:

1. *Photos and illustrations* should be used on the cover rather than simply typography. An all-type cover cannot convey any desirable image but that of dignity. This may suffice for the few companies that are so well known that their name alone conjures up the proper image in the mind of the reader. Unfortunately, most companies are not in this position.

2. *Use people* in illustrations and photographs appearing on annual covers—preferably people using a company product. Pictures without action stifle the reader's desire to open the report.

3. *A brief, carefully worded "headline"* on the cover will help develop the message of the cover photograph or illustration and make the point the company is trying to put across more meaningful.

4. *Keep annual report cover simple.* Not only is this the key to good layout, it is the basis for good communications.

Financial Highlights.   This section should be one of the first items that a stockholder sees when he opens the report. However, to be effective, highlights must be highlights only. Beyond a certain point, the more information presented, the less readership the section will receive. The number of items should probably be kept to no more than ten meaningful figures. Comparisons with the previous year, along with percentage changes, should also be listed.

Among the items that can be included in this section are:

1. Sales
2. Earnings before taxes
3. Taxes on income
4. Earnings after taxes
5. Profit margin
6. Earnings per share
7. Dividends per share
8. Number of shares outstanding
9. Equity per share
10. Return on stockholder equity

President's Letter. The president's letter should be an honest discussion of the past year, both its good and bad aspects. Otherwise, the stockholder's credibility will be strained, reversing the entire effect that the company is trying to achieve. There are several ways of getting conviction into the president's letter:

1. *Writing style:* When the president's letter is written in a man-to-man tone rather than in a legalistic fashion the reader will more easily accept what he reads. This approach demands short words, short sentences, and a short message.

2. *Admission of problems:* It is shortsighted to attempt to gloss over unfavorable results or ignore an important company problem—especially when such an event is reflected in the corporate statistics printed elsewhere in the report. It makes much more sense for a company president to admit in his letter that such a situation exists. An open admission of a problem allows a president to tell his stockholders that the company recognizes the problem and to explain how it will be solved. This calms stockholders and puts the company in an excellent position in the eyes of the financial community: Management

not only had the ability to recognize the problem, it had the strength to report it and has the know-how to solve it.

3. *Length:* The president's letter should be short, preferably one page; it should omit details that can be handled better in other sections of the report.

4. *Reference to ownership situation:* The use of phrases like "your company" or "your management" have a false ring. A stockholder who owns 100 shares of a company is well aware of the extent of his participation. Using patronizing phrases can create the opposite reaction to the one the company is trying to achieve. Substituting "our company" implying ownership by all stockholders, including management, gives a truthful, realistic and believable impression.

Feature Section.   The details of a company's operations should follow the President's Letter. This section should report more than *what* occurred during the past year. It also should *explain* the events that occurred and help the reader to *evaluate* them.

The annual report should always include—every year—an explanation of the company's business. A company should not be afraid to repeat salient points in each annual report. Many executives mistakenly assume that because information was printed in a previous report, it was read and remembered by stockholders and analysts. These executives forget that although they have referred to the annual report frequently during the previous 12 months, few analysts and almost no stockholders have done so. In addition, during any year a company acquires many new stockholders who have never read its annual report.

The smaller the company, the more information its annual report should contain about its operations, products, and industry, since the smaller the company, the less the analyst—or the stockholder—is liable to know about it. One reason for this lack of familiarity with smaller companies is the large number of reports issued annually. Each analyst probably receives annual reports from hundreds of companies, the majority of them arriving at about the same time each year. Most of these reports will be filed for possible future reference, but it is apparent that the analyst cannot take the time to read and study the reports from any but the largest companies in his field of specialization. Therefore, when he does refer to an annual report, he should learn enough from it to provide him with detailed information about the company, its products, and the industries it serves as well as what occurred during the past year.

The Feature Section can generally be divided into three separate areas: the Financial Review, Divisional Reviews, and Special Activity Reviews. There is a great deal of flexibility as to which items appear under each section, depending on a company's internal organizational pattern.

FINANCIAL REVIEW. This section will normally contain discussions of such items as sales, earnings, taxes, financial position, non-recurring items, inventory position, dividends, cash flow, and capital expenditures and requirements.

In addition to these points, there are two more items that ought to be included in the annual report—the first because it is a convenience to the analyst, the second because it is a convenience for both stockholder and analyst:

1. *Breakdown of sales and earnings by quarter:* These should include percentage changes from the prior year. While it is true that the analyst has received each quarterly report as it was published, chances are that these interim reports have become buried deep in the analyst's files. Since the annual report is a permanent document of record—a publication that the analyst will usually keep within convenient reach—such quarterly statistics have a place in the annual report.

2. *Dividend-payments summary by quarters:* Again, since the annual report is a corporate "history"—a permanent document of record—a dividend summary should be presented that includes record date, payment date, and rate of dividend per share. Apart from being helpful and convenient to the analyst, the dividend summary will help a stockholder determine

whether or not he received all dividends due him, and aid him in filing his income-tax return.

DIVISIONAL REVIEW.   The review of the company's divisions or products is where the reader should be told how the company operates. Naturally, the events of the past year should be reported, but in addition, the company should try to give the reader a proper perspective of its operations. For example, information should be included about the company's products —such as the total market, market penetration, marketing techniques, and competitive factors—about major economic variables that affect the company, and about new product potential, rather than just a description of a new product.

SPECIAL ACTIVITY REVIEW.   Sections on manufacturing, research, management structure, and other company activities are usually included under this review. Each topic should be made meaningful for the reader. For example, it is not enough to mention a $3 million, 200,000 square foot plant expansion. The effects of the expansion on total capacity, product mix, and efficiency are necessary to make the figures relevant.

Research activities should be discussed in terms that most readers will understand. Unfathomable scientific terminology may impress a reader but will not give him an insight into what the company is doing.

Illustrations.   Good pictures have additional benefits beyond being attractive. They can tell a story. Thus, pictures must not only attract, but inform as well. Pictures that fail to catch the reader—such as photographs of factory buildings or plain product illustrations—should be improved, from a dramatic point of view, or be shunted aside to make room for more interesting material. One way to perk up a picture is to put people in the scene. And—to add still more reader interest— those people should be doing something. People portrayed sitting, standing, or simply staring, add little to a photograph.

Captions.   Illustrations not only stop the reader who is turning pages, but get him to read the text below. Thus, captions appearing under photographs and charts offer management a unique, easy, and constant medium for image building throughout the pages of the annual report. Most captions are mere labels that describe only what is seen in the photo. A good caption has the company's "message" written into it.

A run-of-the-mill caption that is simply a label turns out this way: "Our new electric screwdriver, pictured above, puts power to work whenever screws must be driven or removed." Compare that caption with the following: "Our company again made a major innovation in the 'do-it-yourself' home tool market with the introduction of this electric screwdriver. New products like this developed in our own research laboratories have helped us achieve a compound growth rate of 20 per cent annually for the past decade."

Other Ways to Improve the Report.

1. *Product information:* Do not forget to list important products. Stockholders are often unaware of the many items produced by a company in which they own stock.

2. *Where stock is traded:* The company should name each exchange where the stock is listed, or state that it is traded over the counter, if that is the case.

3. *Statistical review:* This financial summary—containing statistics for at least 10 years—should be spread over two pages with sufficient space between lines and rows to have each item stand by itself. Otherwise it becomes too difficult to read.

4. *Use charts:* They can often tell a financial story better than numbers or descriptive text. Charts should be clearly labeled and selected to illustrate the financial items that are the most pertinent to the company's story. The best chart depicts one specific item. A complicated chart provides too much information, is more confusing than helpful.

5. *Use large type:* A study conducted by the New York Stock Exchange found that almost 17 per cent of all stockholders are 65 years of age or older. Consequently, the size of the type that is used should be large enough for this age group to be able to read without difficulty.

16

The Annual Stockholders' Meeting

There was a day not too long ago when companies intentionally conducted brief, dull, often aloof annual meetings in some obscure, inaccessible small town. Stockholders who managed to overcome the obstacles and attend the meeting were made to feel that they were intruders. Today, however, most companies have learned it is bad business to try purposely to avoid their stockholders. Most meetings are now designed to attract stockholder attendance, and when the stockholder arrives he is made to feel welcome. If he cannot come, he will probably be sent a post-meeting report (see Chapter 14) so that the company will not entirely miss the opportunity to let him know what it told others in his absence.

Enlightened companies see the annual meeting today not as a forum called together by charter and law but as another opportunity to improve their stockholder relations. They see the meeting as a rare chance for management to talk in person with the company's stockholders—always interested ones, since those attending voluntarily chose to do so; to give the stockholder a better understanding of the company and its plans, progress, and problems; to show the stockholder the products the company makes; to answer stockholder questions; and, finally, to clear up stockholder misconceptions.

All in all, the annual meeting is an important event in a company's financial relations program—far more important than indicated by the small proportion of the company's stockholders that actually attend any one meeting.

Unfortunately, many companies do not reap the benefits they should from an annual meeting. There are three major problems striking at the effectiveness of an annual meeting. Two of the three problems are intrinsic in the size of the company. The third problem hits at both the large and small company.

1. *For larger companies:* An annual meeting can easily evolve into an unruly showcase for publicity-seeking professional stockholders who may succeed in making management come off second best.

2. *For smaller companies:* An annual meeting can develop into a meaningless formality with only a handful of stockholders present who listen quietly to the proceedings and then depart.

3. *For all companies:* An annual meeting can become a listless session that completely misses the opportunity to communicate to the stockholders.

Consequently, the following discussion has three purposes: (1) to show larger companies some of the means of maintaining control of the meeting in the face of professional stockholder opposition and confusion, (2) to show smaller companies how they might increase stockholder attendance and participation, and (3) to help all companies inject enthusiasm and interest into the meeting.

CONTROLLING THE LARGE ANNUAL MEETING

An annual meeting gets out of hand and becomes disorganized, time wasting, and aggravating for everyone when the professional stockholder is permitted to dominate the meeting. Once in control of the microphone, many professional stockholders:

1. Ask endless questions to the exclusion of other stockholders who wish to be heard
2. Give long speeches
3. Try to draw the chairman into a debate
4. Make comments that are not germane to the meeting
5. Demand to have the meeting conducted under their rules rather than those set by the chairman

Since the professional stockholder represents the main threat to a well-attended meeting, a company should face up to the problem long before the meeting. There are many things that must be accomplished—before and during the meeting— to keep the professional stockholder and the entire meeting under control. All require planning and work.

Before the Meeting. The pre-meeting planning involves understanding the professional stockholder, learning what changes he earnestly seeks, anticipating his questions, drawing up an agenda to guarantee an orderly progression from topic to topic, and determining the rules under which the meeting is to be conducted.

UNDERSTANDING THE PROFESSIONAL STOCKHOLDER. As the champion of the rights of the small stockholder, the professional stockholder has been valuable to corporations and to stockholders. Many of the things for which the professional has fought during the past quarter-century have become accepted as normal today. The practices that companies have instituted for dealing with their stockholders, and would not now eliminate even if they could, were generally unrecognized until professional stockholders fought for them.

Now that they have achieved most of their goals, many of their actions seem unnecessary. The crusade by the original small group of professional stockholders is now over. Even if many of them do not realize it, they have accomplished what they set out to do. What they are fighting for now is insignificant in terms of what they have accomplished in the past.

Unfortunately, their success, which has been widely publicized, has attracted a band of publicity seekers who use the annual meetings as a vehicle for the satisfaction of their own egos. Rather than championing the rights of small stockholders, they are now more interested in having themselves heard and seeing their names in print. It is with this latter group that companies must use strong measures of control to be sure that they do not dominate meetings.

ANTICIPATING QUESTIONS. An excellent idea of the kinds of questions that may be asked by stockholders, professional or otherwise, can be obtained from the following sources:

1. *Professional stockholder objectives:* Thanks to statements made and published by professional stockholders, management knows the broad range of objectives these men seek. Some of their objectives are:

—To demand the holding of annual meetings in convenient locations
—To urge better and more informative annual reports and better post-meeting reports
—To see that all directors are stockholders in the corporation
—To campaign for increased recognition of preemptive rights for owners
—To keep watch over executive compensation, options, and pensions
—To promote cumulative voting for electing directors
—To eliminate electing directors by the stagger system whereby only a portion of the directors come up for re-election in any one year

2. *The American Society of Corporate Secretaries:* This association publishes "Management Guide to Stockholder Queries at Annual Meetings," which lists 51 pages of questions that might be asked at any annual meeting. It is a thorough compendium that every company can use as a check list.

3. *Stockholder correspondence:* During the course of the year, stockholders may have written to the company requesting information. There is always the likelihood that some of these same questions will be asked at the annual meeting.

4. *Security analysts' questions:* Many of the questions that security analysts ask of management mirror the questions that

stockholders want answered and may ask at the annual meeting.

DRAWING UP AN AGENDA. A list of each item to be covered, and the sequence and method of handling it, should be developed in advance. Adhering to this agenda will help the chairman do everything in a logical sequence and will keep the meeting from becoming disorganized. The highlights of the agenda should be distributed to stockholders or read to them at the beginning of the meeting. If this is done, it will be much easier to get stockholders' cooperation in holding questions and comments until the proper time.

MEETING PROCEDURES. Professional stockholders frequently insist that meetings be run on a democratic basis—generally in accordance with *Robert's Rules of Order.* However, the democratic theory as applied to corporations is not necessarily valid. Law courts, for example, have never held that parliamentary rules should prevail at annual meetings. On the contrary, courts have insisted only that the chairman conduct the annual meeting "in good faith" and "fairly" and that the chairman allow stockholders a "reasonable" right to speak.

It is dangerous to accede to a demand that *Robert's Rules* be employed, simply because the professional stockholder probably is far better versed in *Robert's Rules* than is a company chairman. Trying to run an annual meeting on a parliamentary basis may result in the meeting's degenerating into a shambles as shouts of "Point of Order" and "Point of Information" ricochet around the room.

During the Meeting. Once the chairman raps the gavel to bring the annual meeting to order, he is on the firing line—in terms of keeping order, maintaining his own personal composure, and seeing that every stockholder is treated fairly. Some of the steps the chairman may take to accomplish those objectives include the following:

1. *Explain to stockholders* at the start the rules under which the meeting is to be conducted.

2. *Act quickly and firmly* in handling questions from the floor. Questions and comments that are not pertinent should

not be tolerated. The chairman should firmly rule such questions out of order and go on to the next question. Any attempt to *half* answer an extraneous question generally results in an impossible hassle.

Questions that are pertinent should be answered forthrightly, even if they touch on sensitive points. It is better to admit a problem exists and discuss what is being done to overcome it than to gloss over a bad situation. Except for information that would help competitors, stockholders are entitled to clear, frank, and courteous answers to proper questions.

3. *Instantly rule out of order* questions about day-to-day management decisions. At all times, the chairman must be unyielding in this respect.

4. *Limit each stockholder,* in advance, to a specific number of questions—with the promise to return to him if time permits. Any stockholder obviously armed with a long list of questions should be made to feel the pressure of others waiting to be heard.

5. *Run the meeting* in accordance with the agenda. When anyone refuses to comply, the chairman should instantly call the sergeant-at-arms and have the individual removed—politely but firmly.

6. *Control each microphone* so that any stockholder's microphone can be summarily turned off when need be. This task may be delegated to an assistant that can easily be signalled. Naturally, no stockholder should ever be allowed to bring to the meeting a portable microphone.

7. *Rule out of order* anyone attempting to speak at times other than the specified time.

8. *Never allow* a stockholder to gain the upper hand by coming up front to address the audience. Kept in the midst of the audience, a domineering stockholder will feel the pressure and antagonism of his fellow stockholders.

INCREASING ATTENDANCE

There are several methods to increase attendance at annual meetings.

Meetings in Major Investment Centers.   The most important step in attracting more stockholders to the annual meeting
is to hold meetings where stockholder interest is. Generally,
stockholders who have sufficient desire to attend meetings will
be found in large cities. A company headquartered in a small
community will usually find its own "backyard" a poor place
to hold an annual meeting.

A geographical stockholder breakdown will determine
where there is a significant concentration of stockholders.
Once that breakdown has been studied, the best meeting place
will usually become apparent. In following years, the president can elect to hold an annual meeting in other cities with
large stockholder populations—further broadening the company's personal contact with its shareowners.

Closed circuit television has enabled a company to hold a
stockholder meeting at one location, yet give other stockholders the opportunity to attend the meeting in a more convenient
city. Radio Corporation of America has used closed-circuit
television to allow stockholders in both Los Angeles and New
York to participate simultaneously in their annual meeting.

Second Invitations.   Every company must send out a formal
notice to all its stockholders advising when and where the
annual meeting is to be held. Unfortunately, the formal notice
makes dull reading; often, it goes unread.

To build up attendance, a more personalized note from the
president should be mailed to each stockholder living in the
area where the next meeting will be conducted inviting him
to the meeting.

The invitation to the stockholder can be as sincere and
direct as this sample note: "Since we are holding our annual
meeting this year not far from where you live, I hope you will
be able to attend. We have some topics on the agenda that
may give you a better insight into our company. The specifics
about the meeting—date, time, and location—appear below.
I am looking forward to meeting you personally."

Even if the stockholder getting such a personal invitation

cannot attend the meeting, he will be favorably impressed by the company's thoughtfulness.

Convenient Location.   The fact that a meeting is conducted in an area with a high stockholder population is no guarantee that large numbers of stockholders will turn out. If the exact site of the meeting is relatively inaccessible, few stockholders will attend. For example, many New York City stockholders who would attend a meeting held in midtown Manhattan, would pass up a meeting if it were held in Long Island City, New York, or Newark, New Jersey, even though they are both within the metropolitan New York area. Thus, management must think in terms of stockholder convenience when picking the site for the meeting. The best place, unquestionably, is at a location in the center of the city.

Although it is usually best to avoid holding meetings at company plants, which are often located in relatively inconvenient industrial areas, a company may sometimes have a new development at its facility that it thinks would interest stockholders. In this case, the company should arrange for transportation to and from the meeting. While this approach toward stockholder convenience will help attract stockholders, it will not gain as many as would attend a meeting held in the center of the city.

Lunch.   The prospects of having lunch at an annual meeting will attract some stockholders who otherwise would not attend. One reason is that a lunch meeting is held at a time that is convenient for many stockholders. Another is that stockholders look at a lunch meeting less as an austere business session and more as an enjoyable social meeting. If an annual meeting is to include lunch, such information should appear in the letter to the stockholders.

Product Gifts.   When practical, a company should give a gift of some of the company products to stockholders who attend the annual meeting. Such a gift does double duty. It pleases the stockholder, since everyone likes to receive a gift, and it enables the stockholder who otherwise might not have come in contact with the product to learn firsthand about some of the things the company makes.

MAKING MEETINGS INTERESTING

The annual meeting is a tool—similar in some respects to the annual report—for communicating with stockholders. How successful the annual meeting is in communicating depends on management's efforts in making the yearly session an effective one.

Many routine annual meetings are dull affairs, often planned by individuals who emphasize complying with legal requirements. There are others that are lively and stimulating to the stockholders. Invariably, these are planned by individuals who understand that stockholders are interested in the company and have come to learn more about it. Information aimed at the stockholder—not money spent on an elaborate meeting—determines the effectiveness of an annual meeting. Stockholders should leave the meeting wanting to attend again the following year.

Successful meetings are characterized by interesting talks by company executives, willingness to answer questions frankly and fully, good displays of the company's products, and illustrations of how the company develops, produces, or markets its products.

The routine part of a meeting should be shortened as much as possible. Reading of the minutes, swearing in judges of election, counting of ballots, and similar items on the agenda are tedious and boring and should be handled in the most expeditious manner legal counsel will permit.

The "hub" of the annual meeting is the president's talk. This is the principal address, and it must be a meaningful one to help stockholders understand how the company operates, not merely a rehash of what was included in the annual report. The talk should contain a brief review of the company's operations, its progress since the annual report was issued, and a discussion of the company's situation, objectives, and plans.

The annual meeting format enables a company to use a variety of communicating techniques that it cannot use in an annual report. This can include motion pictures, live models, television commercials, product demonstrations—whatever is necessary to tell the company's story to the stockholders.

Bausch & Lomb, Inc., used a technique that helped make its meeting interesting as well as informative. The company demonstrated on each of the stockholders present a new device it hoped to sell which would screen large groups of people for eye care. Fifty-six per cent of Bausch & Lomb stockholders attending the meeting were quickly informed that they needed glasses.

17

The Financial Press

Management too often conducts its financial relations program with undue emphasis on the number of newspaper clippings it amasses each month. One reason for this is the mistaken belief that the force that motivates most investors to buy stock is the articles they read about a company in the financial pages of a newspaper or magazine. Printed stories about a company do not, in themselves, stimulate most investors to make stock purchases. Except as it stimulates those "in-and-out" investors who buy a stock for a quick trade, generally the most a favorable story in the financial press will do is one of the following:

1. Cause some investors to ask their brokers' opinion on the stock (However, to give his opinion on most stocks, the broker usually will find it necessary to consult his research department, and it is there that the basic investment decisions will be determined.)
2. Reinforce to the company's current stockholders the value of their investment
3. Stimulate stock-buying action on the part of investors who had been thinking of buying the stock before they read the article but had not yet reached a decision

In perspective, a financial press program is only one—and one of the least important—component of a well-conducted investor relations program.

One reason for the overemphasis on financial press articles is that there are executives who enjoy "making the *Times*" or "hitting the *Wall Street Journal*." A more important reason is that newspaper clippings are tangible objects that management can see, count, display and paste in a scrapbook. Clippings are proof that something is being done constructively, while it is virtually impossible for management to measure with a specific yardstick the work done with security analysts and stockholders. Although newspaper clippings may seem to some to be the true measure of an investor relations program, it is really the effectiveness of the day-to-day liaison with security analysts that spells the difference between a good and a poor investor relations program.

Nevertheless, articles and stories in the financial press do give a company an opportunity to communicate—through an outside and disinterested party—with its stockholders, potential stockholders, and members of the professional investment community. The information obtained from published stories can result in the development of strong positive or negative attitudes about a company; the impression a company projects will depend in part on its press policies and practices.

Considering financial press relations in its proper perspective —important, but not overridingly so—this chapter will explain the policies necessary to carry out a good program.

MAINTAINING GOOD PRESS RELATIONS

There is obviously more involved in working with the financial press than simply issuing an occasional press release. This is a specialized function and must be handled by experts who understand precisely how the press works, who know what it will accept, and who are able to get information to it in the best manner and at the right time.

Press Relations Staff and Company Spokesmen. Good press relations depends on either an internal or external qualified press relations staff. Such a staff must have a thorough knowledge of company policy and must have management's authority to speak for the company and to answer questions on behalf of the company. Furthermore, management itself must select top executives who will be permitted to speak for the company. Typically, they are the same men designated to talk with security analysts; occasionally, however, an executive in charge of a specialized department may be assigned to discuss his operation with the press when detailed information is needed.

Executives designated as company spokesmen must be able to state their position on any situation they are discussing with authority and accuracy. Top-management spokesmen should be available to answer questions from the press directly when any news release contains areas of controversy. However, routine questions can be handled by the public relations staff once management has approved a news release.

Press Relations Policy. Once management has settled on the individuals who may and may not talk with the press, the *policy* problems of dealing with the press should be outlined. Among the foundations of any company's press relations policies should be the following:

OBJECTIVITY. Each press announcement should set a tone of objectivity and imply that the company wants to keep the public adequately informed. No press release should contain promotional adjectives that lead the reader to suspect that stock touting rather than financial disclosure is at the root of the announcement.

HONESTY. No press announcement should imply things that are not completely true nor omit information that might have a negative connotation.

A reporter's questions must always be answered honestly. Aside from any consideration of virtue or morality, a dishonest answer may ultimately jeopardize the company's future relations with the press. This is especially true when the answer to a question does not reflect favorably on the company. Hiding or evading the question frequently piques the reporter's curiosity—prompts him, perhaps, to get his answer from another source, one less favorable to the company. If management answers even the difficult questions with candor, the reporter will usually accept the answer for what it is and put it in its proper context.

No "OFF-THE-RECORD" COMMENTS. Management should never say anything off the record that it does not want to see in print. Certainly, many journalists will keep an off-the-record remark in confidence, but, unfortunately, other reporters will take such comments and attribute them *in print* to "industry observers," or "insiders," or "Wall Streeters." Thus, while the company is not credited with having made the disclosure, the secret is nonetheless publicized.

CONSISTENCY. Management should answer all questions in the same manner, but need not answer the same question from different reporters in the same depth. This is because the amount of detail needed by some publications differs markedly from that needed by others, and the importance of some financial publications does not justify the expenditure of as many executive hours as does that of others. As with security analysts, financial writers have differing degrees of importance to a company. However, an enterprising reporter who has the ability to ask penetrating questions or to probe into areas that others overlook is obviously entitled to receive non-confidential information that others do not ask about.

Press Conferences. Press conferences should be held to a minimum. They are time-consuming, both to company executives and to the members of the financial press, and usually are not necessary. Press conferences can be justified when a company is announcing (1) a *major* story, (2) a new development that requires a physical demonstration, or (3) a story that is so complex or so controversial that there are bound to be more questions asked than any press release could possibly anticipate.

Scheduling Directors' Meetings. To get the greatest benefit from the news that results from actions taken by directors—and a good portion of company announcements originate this way—it is the best policy to schedule directors' meetings with newspaper deadlines in mind. The best newspaper coverage can usually be obtained when announcements are made early in the day. An announcement late in the day is almost impossible to get into the afternoon newspapers and it is sometimes difficult to get good coverage from morning newspapers under the pressure of their deadlines.

Companies that hold late afternoon directors' meetings so that announcements can be made after the 3:30 p.m. New York Stock Exchange closing often cheat themselves out of good newspaper coverage. If news is to be released when the New York stock markets are closed, it is better to try to do it before the 10 a.m. opening.

Another factor to be considered is the day on which directors meet. Meetings on Monday through Thursday are best. Friday directors' meetings usually mean news in Saturday newspapers, which have much lower readership than weekday papers.

TIMELY DISCLOSURE

News is today's information—not yesterday's and sometimes not even that of an hour ago. Much of the news emanating from corporations has an immediate bearing on decisions being made by the investment public; news concerning sales and earnings, dividend changes, strikes, and major new-product developments are but a few of the items that may shape the investment community's judgments. To delay such vital stories, then, for even a few hours may, in certain instances, do an injustice to the entire financial community. The listing agreement of the New York Stock Exchange contains the following comments concerning *timely* disclosures:

In addition to the reports specifically provided for, prompt release should be made whenever there are important developments which might affect security values or influence investment decisions of stockholders or the investing public. For example, the listing agreement requires immediate publicity in respect of dividend action or the omission of such action. This is a matter which affects security values and because it is a universal occurence it is possible to prescribe for it, specifically, in the listing agreement. On the other hand, discovery of oil on the properties of a manufacturing company, or development of a new product which may affect profits substantially, or any one of a number of other possible occurrences too numerous and varied for specific definition in the listing agreement, may have an even greater effect on security values and be just as needful of prompt publicity.

It goes without saying, of course, that the bad news should be disclosed just as promptly and as fully as the good, and it may be worth saying that few things are more damaging to stockholder relations and the general public regard for corporate securities than information withheld, whether by inadvertence or by policy. That is not difficult to understand when, as a result of the inadvertence or policy, people may be paying more, or selling for less, than securities are worth at the moment on the basis of the known but unannounced developments.[1]

Any company—whether listed on the Big Board or not—that does not adhere to a policy of prompt and full disclosure can expose itself to legal action as well as create a poor relationship with the entire financial community.

Dividends. Announcements of dividends must be made to the press immediately after they have been declared by the directors and even before those directors have left the meeting. To expedite the release of dividend news, dividend action should be placed early on the board's agenda.

A specific officer present at the meeting should be designated to see that the Dow-Jones news service and other news media are notified immediately following the dividend action taken by the directors. The actual releasing of the dividend announcement should be coordinated with the company's public relations counsel or internal staff. These specialists can get the news out more quickly and to a wider audience if the announcement procedures are arranged with them ahead of time.

Whenever a company that has established a pattern of declaring a dividend at regular intervals is suddenly about to interrupt that pattern, an announcement to that effect must be made. Not to issue news of such a change can only result in uncertainty on the part of present and potential stockholders. An-

---

[1] New York Stock Exchange, *Company Manual.* Reprinted by permission.

nouncement of a postponement of a dividend declaration should be made as soon as this decision has been reached.

When the directors change a regular dividend rate or declare an extra or a stock dividend, the announcement should make it clear that a change has been made and specify the nature of the change. In the case of a change in the regular dividend rate, the company should report the previous rate. When extra dividends and stock dividends are reported, the company should indicate whether a similar action was taken in the prior year.

Unfavorable News.   Every company at some time will be faced with the necessity of making an announcement that can only be classified as unfavorable news. The way such information is issued can have an important bearing on how it is received. The best approach to unfavorable news is to release it quickly and in detail as full as possible. This brings the facts into the open and avoids rumors that might exaggerate the situation.

For example, if a company's sales and earnings in a forthcoming period are going to be poor, the company should reveal this information immediately. An interview with a publication such as the *Wall Street Journal* can disseminate this information quickly and widely. The result may be a sharp adjustment in the price of the company's stock, but it will usually be a prompt one. Once the news is out there is nothing further to discount. If the news is not disseminated promptly, the price of the company's stock will start a long, gradual erosion—perhaps beyond the level that might have occurred if the news had been handled forthrightly—as word of unfavorable developments leaks out.

Coping with Rumors.   When rumors concerning factual information circulate on Wall Street, then (see the discussion on page 215) pre-disclosure is vital. But rumors are not limited to factual information; indeed, most of them are distortions of fact. When untrue rumors become widespread and perhaps affect the stock's action, the New York Stock Exchange, in its listing agreement, recommends the following procedure:

Occasions may also arise when rumors have been circulated which have no basis in fact or which require clarification or interpretation and which also result in unusual activity or price changes in a particular security. Under such circumstances, the most effective procedure is the quick and speedy denial of such rumors through a release to the public Press. Immediate and direct notice or clarification should also be given to the Department of Stock List at the Exchange.[2]

Premature Announcements. Naturally, management often knows in advance of a development that it does not yet wish to announce. For example, while preliminary acquisition discussions are under way, management's policy usually is one of absolute secrecy. It is often impossible, however, to keep such discussions a secret simply because scores of individuals usually are brought into the situation before final action is determined. In the case of the acquisition, for example, a tabulation of executives, directors, auditors, and attorneys representing both companies *plus* secretaries who type the correspondence and agreements (not to mention wives and others who should not have been told) will undoubtedly reveal that some 50 to 60 individuals are privy to this "closely guarded secret."

Consequently, news about forthcoming company events often leaks out *despite* an honest attempt to keep the subject under wraps. When the secret starts to spread through Wall Street, the company may be forced to disclose information before it is prepared to do so. As a guideline, the listing agreement of the New York Stock Exchange contains the following comments on pre-disclosure of a news announcement:

Unusual market activity in a security accompanied by a substantial price change has on occasion occurred shortly before the announcement of an important corporate action or development. Such incidents are extremely embarrassing and damaging to both the company and the Exchange since the public may quickly conclude that someone acted on the basis of "inside" information.

Acquisitions, mergers, stock splits, changes in dividend rates or earnings, new contracts, products or discoveries are the type of development most likely to be involved. Frequently, these matters require discussion and study by corporate officials before final decisions can be made. The extreme care which must be used in keeping such studies and discussions on a confidential basis is evident. The market action of a company's securities should be closely watched at a time when consideration is being

[2] *Ibid.*

given to such matters, so that if the occasion should arise the company would be prepared to make a public announcement of the matter under consideration.

There have been instances in the past where it became necessary for a company to make such a public announcement of a matter it was preparing for presentation to its Board of Directors. Obviously, such an action places the Board, which must exercise judgement on the proposal, in an embarrassing and undesirable position.

In view of the importance of this matter and the potential difficulties involved, the Exchange respectfully suggests that a periodic review be made of the manner in which confidential information is handled by listed companies.[3]

[3] *Ibid.*

18

Surveying Investor Attitudes

PROBLEMS AND BENEFITS OF ATTITUDE SURVEYS

The way to determine the effectiveness of a company's investor relations program is to check regularly the attitudes of the investment community. The investment community, in this regard, includes the professional security analyst, the company's stockholders, and investors in general. Surveying investor opinions shows a company what must be done to overcome the wrong impressions and to reinforce Wall Street's accurate assessments.

Lack of Consistent Research Programs. Few managements have made any attempt to evaluate the effectiveness of their current program. On the contrary, most of them conduct their financial and stockholder relations programs on a seat-of-the-pants basis. Investor relations programs usually are determined by an executive's "feel" of the situation or by his peering over someone's shoulder to see what others are doing.

Companies that would not consider introducing a new product without prior market testing, running an advertisement that was not pre-tested, or permitting a change in an established product without first surveying consumers go on year after year without trying to learn anything about the effectiveness of their financial and stockholder relations program. Only a few scattered companies—such giants as the General Electric Company, International Business Machines Corporation, Standard Oil Company (New Jersey), and American Telephone and Telegraph Company—are doing research on a regular basis in the field of financial and stockholder relations.

One reason that so little use is made of investor research surveys is their high cost *in relation to the overall investor relations budget.* Of course, companies rarely figure the cost of the time that their top executives devote to financial and stockholder relations programs when the budget is being determined. If they did include such high expenses, the proportionate cost of research would drop sharply.

Another understandable reason why management may be reluctant to probe Wall Street's opinion of the company is that the findings of the survey reflect directly on management's capabilities. Surveys may show, for example, that investors regard a company as unimaginative, unaggressive, or even unreliable —characteristics that few managements would want to hear, let alone believe.

Benefits of Surveys.   Regardless of the monetary or psychological motivations, the unfortunate consequence of not surveying Wall Street's opinions is that management has an inadequate picture of them. If the realistic, cold-blooded information of how Wall Street views the company does *not* get back to management, the company will not change its program—which means that in some cases it unwittingly will be perpetuating an image with which it disagrees.

Once a company realizes, however, that Wall Street views it inaccurately, then it can launch a campaign to reshape itself in the Street's eyes. That realization can come about only through a formal, well-planned survey program.

While all publicly owned companies need to keep tabs on Wall Street's feelings towards them, companies that are *changing*—diversifying their products, entering new and competitive markets, acquiring other firms, going international—need to be especially sensitive to how the investment community is reacting. This is so because Wall Street frequently takes a long time to digest the message that corporate changes are taking place. It is quite possible for a company to enter into new and quite different fields that take it out of its original industry and still be tagged *years later* with the same old attributes. Regular testing will show the changing company how much of its new character Wall Street has accepted and how much educating remains to be done.

Preliminary Objective Self-appraisal.   Before any survey can be launched, management must determine what kind of company it is running. In order to evaluate Wall Street's opinion, it must have its own honest answers to such questions as: Are we the leader in our field? Are we really progressive? Do we tend to be conservative? Do we launch new products well above the industry average? Are we strong in research? Do we follow the crowd? Is management young? Are we beset with labor difficulties?

The task of self-assessment is not an easy one. Typically, the vice president of sales will view the company differently than will the financial vice president. And the vice president of operations will, in turn, have a still different view of the company.

In the areas where both management and Wall Street agree on the corporate image, there is no problem, but in the areas where discrepancies occur—the company thinks of itself as a leader, the investment community does not—management can concentrate on proving to Wall Street that its assessment is inaccurate. Such a concentrated effort to change Wall Street's attitude should be undertaken only when that attitude is actually wrong. Wall Street will not be taken in for long—if at all—by a misrepresentative image urged by the company.

KINDS OF SURVEYS

There are several kinds of surveys a company can use to plumb Wall Street's reactions. Management can zero in on a communication tool—the annual report, for example—and make it the subject of a survey aimed at security analysts, asking such questions as: What sections of the report did you read? Why? What sections of the report did you skip over? Why? What message did you get by looking at the cover? Were there enough statistical breakdowns for you? Did the charts help you understand the statistics? Was your overall impression of the report favorable or unfavorable?

Or, a company might query its stockholders on the annual meeting with questions similar to these: Why did you come to the meeting? Are you glad that you came? Were the talks informative? What was the best part of the entire meeting for you? Do you plan to attend next year's annual meeting? Why?

External Measurements. Many aspects of a financial relations program can be tested relatively simply without special surveys. For example, the number of shares traded daily can easily be checked to see what progress is being made in increasing market activity. Or the multiple at which a company's stock sells in relation to its competitors will give management some idea of the esteem in which the company is held by the financial community.

Internal Surveys. A company can get a good look at a *portion* of its image through internal analysis—a checking of certain statistics that are available in the company's own records. A study of those records will reveal both professional investor and stockholder attitudes.

PROFESSIONAL INVESTORS. Answers to the following questions are available within the company:

1. *How many analysts call the company?* If records are kept of these calls, it is easy to determine the amount of professional investor interest the company is generating.

2. *How many brokerage reports are written?* This tabulation

should include both comprehensive analyses of the company and one-paragraph mentions by brokers.

3. *How many institutions own stock, and how many shares are owned by these institutions in relation to similar companies or in relation to the number of shares available for trading?* The answers will quickly tell management whether or not the company is attractive to institutions. Institutional ownership statistics give management the opportunity to ask itself: "Are we really getting our fair share?"

STOCKHOLDERS. Analysis of the following data will give management useful information on stockholder attitudes:

1. *The number of stockholders:* A charting of that statistic will show whether a company has been gaining or losing stockholders.

2. *The geographic spread of those stockholders:* Results of these findings will reveal whether or not a company's list is overly weighted in a particular region compared with general geographic patterns of investor ownership.

3. *Stockholder turnover rate:* This statistic—based on the ratio of the number of new stockholders to total stockholders—will tell management whether or not its stockholders are loyal to the company. Or from another point of view, it will highlight the speed with which stockholders become disenchanted with management.

4. *Shareowners' rank by number of shares:* This breakdown will show a company whether its securities appeal more to the small owner or to the large investor. Such information is important in helping management shape its communications to the shareowners.

5. *Number of proxies returned:* A decline in the percentage of proxies returned—or votes cast—should alert management to a change that may be occurring in the attitude of stockholders towards the company.

6. *Analysis of proxy vote:* The percentage of votes cast against management or its proposals gives a statistical record each year of the stockholders' reaction to the company.

Outside Research Findings. Some independent organizations from time to time conduct broad research investigations
into specific areas involving stockholders and the investment
community. Among them are the New York Stock Exchange,
Corplan Associates, Opinion Research Corporation, and Merrill
Lynch, Pierce, Fenner & Smith. Their findings can sometimes be
applied to analysis of a company's program.

For example, if stockholders in the over-65 age bracket com-
prise 17 per cent of the holders of companies listed on the Big
Board, this information can be used as a yardstick against which
a company can evaluate its own comparable statistics. Thus, if
a company discovers that its over-65 stockholder group makes
up 30 per cent of the total, it can assume that it appeals to eld-
erly investors. Depending on the company's objectives, this may
or may not be a negative point.

Similar comparisons can be used to check a company's stockholders against overall stockholder patterns in terms of income,
occupation, sex, education, and geographic location.

Surveying Wall Street. To discover how Wall Street views
the company, management must set about to survey both the
non-professional audience (the company's stockholders) and
the professional audience (the security analysts who follow the
company).

STOCKHOLDER SURVEYS. There are several types of surveys
that a company can use to determine attitudes of its stockholders. They are:

1. *Mail surveys:* These are the easiest and least costly way of
researching the largest number of stockholders. In a mail survey
the questions should be limited in number and kept simple. The
number of responses from stockholders generally is extremely
high for questionnaires of this type, which makes the survey
more reliable and usable than most results from this kind of poll.

2. *Telephone surveys:* This type of interview gives the company an opportunity to question stockholders in greater detail
than do mail surveys. Stockholders are in general quite coopera-

tive when called and asked questions by a representative of a company in which they have an investment.

3. *Personal interviews:* The most information can be obtained by using personal interviews. These are most costly and require considerably more preparation than do the other types of surveys. However, they may be the only practical way to obtain certain kinds of detailed information. In addition to trained interviewers—either on the staff of the company or an outside research organization—some companies have their executives call on a small number of stockholders each year to enable them to get a first hand reaction to what stockholders think of, and expect from, the company.

SECURITY ANALYST SURVEYS. The same types of surveys used for stockholders—mail, telephone, and personal interviews— can also be used in researching attitudes among security analysts. The professional investment community is the most influential factor in determining the attitudes of investors towards the company and it is the easiest group to survey.

Fortunately, the professional financial community is small when compared with the number of non-professional investors. And for practical purposes, the attitudes of only a small per cent of this professional group are important to the company. It is the relatively few opinion leaders specializing in a company's industry who are the major influence on how the rest of the financial community feels. Research efforts directed toward this relatively small group frequently can uncover the reasons for the attitude of the *entire* professional investment community. A survey of security analysts can determine not only what security analysts know and think about a company, but what they know and think about a company in relation to other companies in the field.

Most opinion research firms do not have the specific intimate knowledge of the investment community to phrase the questions properly or select the proper respondents. Surveying the investment community requires the assistance of financial relations specialists.

Interviews with security analysts are best conducted by personnel from an outside organization rather than staff personnel. Many analysts would like their replies to be kept confidential—particularly if they are critical of management—and would feel more secure if they were talking to someone not on the company staff.

Any research to determine the attitudes of the professional financial community must be conducted among the right members of the community. Some surveys in the past have sought information from the wrong individuals: partners of brokerage houses not directly concerned with stock research; clerks from proxy departments; security analysts specializing in unrelated industries; and traders and others with no need to have more than a superficial knowledge about the company under study.

On balance, the right people to be surveyed are those who are expected to know the company: typically, the analysts who follow the company's industry. But the exact people to be queried in any survey depend on what questions are being asked. For example, it is apparent that when a company wants to know why it does not have more stockholders on the West Coast, security analysts working on the West Coast must be questioned. And when management wants to know how institutions regard the company, management must query analysts in the research departments of institutions and analysts at brokerage firms that deal heavily with institutions.

Index

effect of convertible securities on
31, 34
effect of repurchasing stock, 40–41,
46
Employee stock ownership
to broaden stock ownership base,
63–64
foreign employees, 63–64
stock repurchased for, 41, 44
Ethical consideration, repurchasing
corporate stock, 46
Exchange of securities to effect repurchase of stock, 43

"Fact Book" or "Information Report," 147
Field trips, for security analysts,
136–38
Films, 184–85
Financial analysts, 109; see also Security analysts
Financial Analysts Federation, directory of members, 152–53
Financial press, 106, 208–16
company spokesmen, 210
dividend announcements, 213–14
effectiveness of articles and stories,
9, 208–09
handling rumors, 214–15
influence on stock buying, 9–10
investors relations program and, 4,
9–10
maintaining good relations, 209–12
premature announcements, 215–16
press conferences, 211
press relations policy, 210–11
scheduling directors' meetings,
211–12
timely disclosures, 212–16
unfavorable news, 214
Financial relations
impact of corporate decisions on,
4–5
investor relations program; see Investor relations program
place in corporate planning, 5,
102–03
Financial relations counsel, 102–10
combining outside and internal
staffs, 109–10
company's chief executive sets policy, 102–03

consultant's staff, 108–09
dealing with security analysts,
117–19
authority of, 118–19
qualifications, 117–18
role of, 118
financial counseling, 106–08
outside consultants, 108–09
advantages of, 103–05
cost of, 104–05
getting the most from, 107
standards for, 107–08
professional investor relations,
105–06
role and function of, 103–08
stockholder relations, 106
Financial writers, 109
Foreign exchange listing, 58–64
to broaden stockholder base, 60–61
choosing, 61–62
guidelines for, 59–60
investor relations abroad, 62–64
opening up new sources of capital,
60
protection against nationalism, 60
Fringe benefits, 41
proxy fights and, 76–77
repurchasing stock for, 41

Haack, Robert W., 52–53

Image, corporate, 219
Industry classifications, effect on
price-earnings ratios, 86–87
Insiders, repurchase of stock by, 46
Institutional investors, 156–64
advantages of, 157–59
assistance in buying and selling,
163–64
attracting attention of, 156, 161–64
disadvantages of, 159–61
mailings to, 163
meetings with, 163
name of nominee holding stock,
153
number and holdings of, 156–57
preference for listed stocks, 50
publicly owned institutions, 161
security analysts on staff, 153
splitting commissions, 57–58
use of brokerage firms specializing
in, 162